SCIENCE ESSENTIALS
BIOLOGY

Food, Blood and Bones

DENISE WALKER

EVANS

LONDON

© Evans Brothers Ltd 2006

Published by:
Evans Brothers
2a Portman Mansions
Chiltern Street
London W1U 6NR

Series editor:
Harriet Brown

Editor:
Katie Harker

Design:
Robert Walster

Illustrations:
Q2A Creative

Printed in China by
WKT Company Limited

British Library Cataloguing in
Publication Data

 Walker, Denise
   Food, blood and bones. - (Science
essentials. Biology)
    1.Nutrition - Juvenile literature
2.Blood - Juvenile
   literature. 3. Bones - Juvenile literature
   I.Title
   572.4

ISBN-10: 0237530147
13-digit ISBN (from 1 January 2007)
978 0 23753014 3

Contents

Introduction

Food is an essential part of our lives. We need to eat regularly to give our bodies energy to carry out life processes. The quantity and the types of food that we eat are also important – vital nutrients help to keep the body in good working order.

This book takes you on a journey to discover more about the importance of diet for good health. Find out about different types of food, learn how food is absorbed into the body and discover the way in which our bones and muscles work together to keep us on the move. You can also find out about famous scientists, like Claudius Galen and William Harvey. Learn how they used their skills to find out how blood transports vital nutrients around the body.

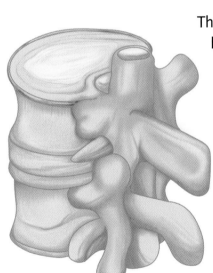

This book also contains feature boxes that will help you to unravel more about the mysteries of diet and health. Test yourself on what you have learnt so far; investigate some of the concepts discussed; find out more key facts; discover some of the scientific findings of the past and see how these might be utilised in the future.

Food is something that many of us take for granted. Now you can understand more about the ways in which a good diet can help to keep us fit and healthy.

DID YOU KNOW?

▶ Watch out for these boxes – they contain surprising and fascinating facts about diet and health.

TEST YOURSELF

▶ Use these boxes to see how much you've learnt. Try to answer the questions without looking at the book, but take a look if you are really stuck.

INVESTIGATE

▶ These boxes contain experiments that you can carry out at home. The equipment you will need is usually cheap and easy to find.

TIME TRAVEL

▶ These boxes describe scientific discoveries from the past, and fascinating developments that pave the way for the advance of science in the future.

ANSWERS

At the end of this book on pages 46 and 47, you will find the answers to questions from the 'Test yourself' and 'Investigate' boxes.

GLOSSARY

Words highlighted in **bold** are described in detail in the glossary on pages 46 and 47.

Eating for life

Food is an essential part of our lives. If you didn't eat or drink your body would be deprived of the energy it needs to grow, maintain and repair itself. Today, the wide variety of foods on display in our supermarkets shows just how many different food types are available. We have a more varied diet than our ancestors, but the quantities in which we eat these foods can affect our health and wellbeing.

YOU ARE WHAT YOU EAT?

Food and fluids are essential to maintain the body's **cells** and to keep fit and well. Your body needs a variety of foods at regular intervals to keep in top condition.

It is important to eat a varied diet because you need to supply your body with all the **nutrients** that it needs. Eating too much (or too little) of one food type can cause **malnutrition**. Malnutrition literally means 'bad feeding' and although this condition is usually associated with underdeveloped parts of the world, malnutrition can affect anyone.

A CLOSER LOOK

What exactly do we mean by a balanced diet? Five basic food groups contain the essential nutrients that the body needs:

▶ Carbohydrates
▶ Proteins
▶ Fats
▶ Vitamins
▶ Minerals

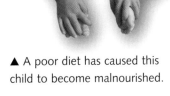

▲ A poor diet has caused this child to become malnourished.

A balanced diet means eating the right proportion of these five food groups (we need to eat more carbohydrates, for example, than vitamins and minerals). Fibre and water are also important parts of a balanced diet. Fibre doesn't provide the body with nutrients but it keeps the digestive system working effectively. Water is one of the most important substances that the body needs. Your cells are mostly made of water and need a constant supply of fluid to work properly. Water also helps to transport materials around the body and to flush out **toxins** that could cause harm.

▲ Eating a variety of foods is the best way to keep healthy.

EATING THE RIGHT STUFF

The following table shows examples of foods that make up a varied diet.

FOOD GROUP	SOURCE
Carbohydrates	Pasta, bread, rice, potatoes
Proteins	Meat, fish, cheese, milk
Fats	Eggs, dairy products, dips and sauces
Vitamins	A – carrots B – egg yolk C – oranges and lemons D – fish oil
Minerals	Iron – liver Calcium – milk Iodine – fish
Fibre	Bran cereals, sweetcorn, celery, tomatoes, cucumber

GETTING THE BALANCE RIGHT

How much food you need to eat depends on your age, your gender and your body size. Larger people need more food because they have more cells to maintain. Men also tend to eat more than women because they have more muscle tissue to sustain (muscles use a lot of energy).

Some governments advise the public about following a healthy diet. In the US and the UK such guidelines include:

▶ Eat at least five portions of fruit and vegetables each day. These can be fresh, frozen, tinned, dried or a glass of juice.

▶ Grill, bake, poach, boil, steam or microwave instead of frying or roasting. Or you could 'dry roast' without adding any fat.

▶ Choose lean meat and trim off the fat and skin.

▶ Eat more starchy foods such as pasta, rice, potatoes, cereals and pulses (beans, peas and lentils). These should make up about a third of your diet.

▶ Try to eat fish at least twice a week. You can eat up to four portions of oily fish a week, such as mackerel, sardines and trout, but avoid having more than this.

▶ Reduce the amount of sugar in your diet.

▶ Don't add salt to your food and be aware of the salt content of ready-prepared foods.

▶ Drink plenty of water each day, especially in hot weather or if you exercise.

▶ It is also important to keep a check on the quantities of food portions in your diet and to take regular physical exercise.

▲ Oily fish, such as sardines, are a good source of proteins, vitamins, minerals and fatty acids that have been found to protect against the risk of heart disease.

TIME TRAVEL: DISCOVERIES OF THE PAST

▶ Scientists have been studying the diets of our early ancestors by looking at fossil remains and analysing ancient hair samples. Their results show that between two and three million years ago, early man also followed a varied diet of fruits, leaves, meat, vegetables and seafood.

Sometimes, eating a balanced diet is not possible due to particular circumstances. Some people follow a special diet for medical or religious reasons. Others choose to follow an alternative diet because of their personal beliefs. In some parts of the world, food is scarce and people have to eat whatever is available.

AVOIDING MEAT

Vegetarians and vegans are now common across the world. Some simply do not like the taste of meat. Others think that animals should not be eaten – perhaps for religious reasons. A vegetarian diet is one where animal meat products are avoided. A vegan diet avoids all products relating to animals, including eggs, cheese and milk. Sometimes, strong vegan principles mean that a person will also avoid animal products that aren't food-related, such as leather bags or shoes.

▲ In Hindu communities, cows are regarded as sacred and beef is not eaten.

Meat provides us with protein, iron (a mineral) and fat, but vegans and vegetarians can eat other things to supplement these food types. Fat can be found in dairy products; protein can be found in dairy products and fish; and iron can be found in green vegetables, such as spinach. Vegans may find it more difficult to follow a balanced diet. They need to eat plenty of legumes (lentils and beans) and nuts to get the protein and fat they need.

◄ Vegetarian dishes are becoming common in western diets because some people choose not to eat meat.

INVESTIGATE

▶ Write a list of all the foods you have consumed in the last 24 hours. Don't forget to include drinks and snacks. Now compare your list to the recommended guidelines. In which areas are you lacking in food types? Do you have too many of some food types?

Although vegetarians and vegans can adapt their diet to include all food groups, there are times when particular care is needed to ensure a healthy lifestyle. For example, during pregnancy a vegetarian or vegan would need to eat more protein to keep themselves and their unborn child healthy.

SLIMMING DIETS

In the western world so many food types are now readily available that many people have difficulty controlling the amount of food that they eat. Eating more food than your body needs can lead to health problems such as **obesity** (see page 15). To curb this problem, special diets have become popular in recent years with people who are trying to lose weight. The 'Atkins diet' for example, is a diet plan composed mainly of fat and protein, with very little carbohydrate. Named after the late Dr Atkins, an American **cardiologist**, the diet claims that eliminating carbohydrates from your diet encourages the body to burn fat and therefore lose weight. Research studies have shown that followers of the diet have lost twice as much weight than those following a low-fat diet. Other weight-reducing diet fashions include a high-fibre eating plan that reduces calorie intake while keeping you feeling full for longer, and the grapefruit diet, which claims that half a grapefruit before every meal provides the body with 'fat-annihilating' **enzymes**.

However, many diets have come under criticism from medical authorities because they are thought to be unhealthy eating regimes. Doctors say that replacing carbohydrates with large quantities of meat, for example, supplies the body with too much fat that can lead to health complications such as high **blood pressure** and heart disease (see page 37).

DID YOU KNOW?

▶ Studies have shown that ethnic minority groups in the UK and USA are more likely to develop diseases such as diabetes and heart disease. Doctors believe that this is linked to poor diet, as well as social conditions. In a study of ethnic minority groups in the UK in 1999, Chinese people were found to have the healthiest diet (eating the most fruit and vegetables), while Bangladeshis ate the most fat and the least vegetables. Cultural and social factors are believed to account for these differences.

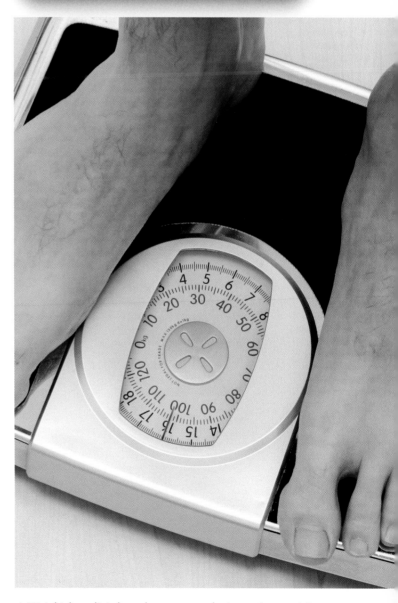

▲ Weight-loss diets have become popular in western society.

Food groups

A balanced diet gives your body the nutrients it needs to carry out important chemical processes. When your body needs more food (or fluid) you will begin to feel hungry (or thirsty). The main food groups provide your cells with the energy they need to carry out vital processes and to keep your body on the move.

CARBOHYDRATES

All living cells release energy when they carry out their daily tasks. This energy comes from a reaction between the food you eat and the oxygen you breathe – a process called **respiration**. We need large quantities of carbohydrates (starch and glucose) in our diet to respire effectively.

Two other types of carbohydrates provide us with energy in a different way. Simple sugars (sometimes called 'refined sugars') provide us with an instant burst of energy that the body uses very quickly. This type of sugar can be found in sweets and chocolate. Simple sugars are a useful energy boost, but they are not the best way to provide a constant supply of energy.

▲ Chocolate provides a burst of energy but tends to make us feel tired a short time later.

Complex carbohydrates are a much better source of energy, capable of nourishing your body over a longer period of time. Complex carbohydrates are found in foods such as pasta and bread.

PROTEINS

Your body needs nutrients from your food to replace worn-out cells and to repair any damage. Proteins are molecules that are made up from smaller parts called amino acids. When protein is consumed it breaks down and then reforms again in human tissue. Proteins also make enzymes – molecules that are needed by all living things to speed up reactions in the body (see page 20). Proteins are found in foods such as meat, fish, cheese and milk.

◀ Pasta contains complex carbohydrates which are a good source of slow-burning energy.

VITAMINS AND MINERALS

Your body needs small amounts of vitamins and minerals to work properly. Minerals are simple chemicals found in most foods. Examples include iron (which helps red blood cells carry oxygen around the body) and calcium (which helps to build strong teeth and bones). Vitamins are more complicated chemicals. A diet lacking in vitamins can cause a range of deficiency diseases.

FATS

Fats are important in our diet because they provide us with energy. Instead of dissolving in our blood like other foods, fats accumulate around tissues and cells so they can be used to maintain cell membranes. Stored fat under the skin is also a good source of insulation.

TEST YOURSELF

▶ Design a table showing the main food groups, their use in the body and problems that an excess or deficiency may cause.

There are two types of fat: saturated fats from animal foods, and unsaturated fats from plant foods. Eating fat in moderation is an important part of a balanced diet. However, unsaturated fats are generally healthier – too many saturated fats can lead to health problems linked to blood circulation and the heart (see page 37).

▶ A lack of vitamin D has caused this boy to develop rickets – a disease that causes the bones to soften and bend as the body grows.

▼ The uses of common vitamins and minerals.

VITAMIN OR MINERAL	EXAMPLE SOURCE	USE	DEFICIENCY
Vitamin A	Carrots, liver	Good vision and healthy skin	Bad night vision and unhealthy skin
Vitamin B1	Yeast, beans, egg yolk	Healthy nerves and growth	Beri-beri*
Vitamin C	Oranges, lemons	Tissue repair and resistance to disease	Scurvy
Vitamin D	Sunlight, fish oil	Strong teeth and bones	Rickets**
Iron (mineral)	Liver, cocoa	Healthy red blood cells	Anaemia
Calcium (mineral)	Milk, green vegetables	Strong teeth and bones	Soft bones
Iodine (mineral)	Fish	Thyroid gland	Goitre***

* Beri-beri is a condition that can damage the heart and nervous system. Symptoms include pain, tingling or loss of sensation in hands and feet, muscle wasting and increased heart rate.
** Rickets is a condition resulting in soft bones that cannot support the weight of a growing body. Symptoms include bone pain, slowed growth in children and increased risk of fractures.
*** Goitre is a condition in which the thyroid gland becomes swollen (a gland situated across the front of the neck, just below the voice box). Symptoms include swallowing and breathing problems.

WATER

Every day your body loses about two litres of water as you breathe, sweat and go to the toilet. Because your cells mostly contain water, fluid makes up about two-thirds of your body. It is important to replace the water that you lose by drinking liquids and eating foods that contain water. Although we can survive for up to 60 days without solid food, we cannot survive for more than a few days without water.

In extreme circumstances (in the aftermath of an earthquake, for example) some people can survive for several days if they have access to water. Health guidelines suggest that we should drink about two litres of water a day to replace the fluids that we have lost. We should also drink more in hotter weather or when we exercise.

FIBRE

Fibre is a substance found mainly in plant matter. Fibre forms an important part of our diet even though we are unable to digest and use it in our bodies. Fibre aids the movement of undigested foods through the body. Without fibre we would not be able to pass faeces comfortably and would quickly become constipated. Research has shown that fibre also contributes towards our general health. Fibre reduces the risk of bowel diseases and has been found to reduce the amount of **cholesterol** in our blood, a fatty material that is caused by eating saturated fats (see page 37). Fibre also makes us feel full for longer which is good for those trying to lose weight. Vegetables, fruit and wholemeal bread are rich in fibre.

◄ Water is one of the most important substances that your body needs.

DID YOU KNOW?

▶ Babies have an area of brown fat around their necks. Very young babies are not able to shiver to keep themselves warm so this brown fat is used when it gets cold. It helps the body to generate heat and maintain a healthy temperature.

▶ Americans used to use the term 'limey' to describe sailors from the UK because they were often seen sucking limes when they came off their ships. This was because the sailors were trying to combat the effects of scurvy – a disease often caused on a long voyage when fresh fruit and vegetables are in short supply. Symptoms of scurvy include joint pain, bruising, receding gums and general weakness.

▶ Scientists have found that what you eat can affect your mood – some nutrients have a direct affect on the brain. Proteins, such as meat, are thought to help you to feel more alert, while carbohydrates are thought to be good for relaxation. Researchers also believe that 'comfort food', which is generally high in fat, helps to suppress stress hormones, making you feel more cheerful. Too much of these foods however, can lead to excessive weight gain.

Energy requirements

Thanks to the energy that we get from carbohydrates and fats we are able to go about our daily lives. But sometimes it can be difficult to get the balance right. If we eat too little we may feel faint and tired; if we eat too much we are in danger of becoming overweight.

MEASURING ENERGY

Next time you go shopping, take a look at the labels on packaged food. You will see that as well as detailing the ingredients and food types that a product contains, the label also indicates the amount of energy that the food provides. Energy from food is described in units called kilojoules (kJ) or kilocalories (kCal). Joules and **calories** are small amounts of energy so we use this larger unit where 1 kJ = 1,000 joules and 1 kCal = 1,000 calories. Nowadays, kilojoules are more commonly used (1 kJ = 0.24 kCal).

Your body uses different amounts of energy when you are active and when you are at rest. When you sleep your body uses about 4 kJ a minute to keep your lungs working, your heart beating and your brain functioning. Walking uses about 20 kJ per minute, running about 40 kJ per minute and more vigorous exercise about 80 kJ per minute.

▶ Food labels outline the amount of energy a product contains as well as the ingredients.

WHAT FOOD TYPES DO WE NEED?

We mainly need to eat carbohydrates to aid the process of respiration (see page 10). When carbohydrates are in short supply, the body burns fats for energy. This explains the basis of many weight-reducing diets (see page 9). If both carbohydrates and fats are in short supply, the body begins to burn proteins for energy. When these proteins are parts of the body itself we say that a person is 'starving'. In underdeveloped parts of the world, where crop failures or war can lead to famine, starvation is a major form of malnutrition with serious side effects.

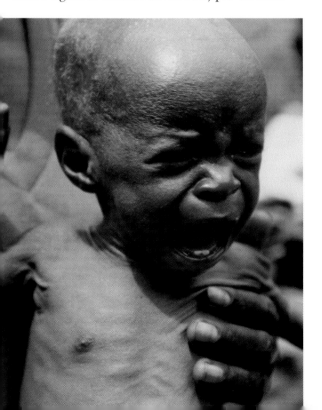

◀ This starving child is at risk of symptoms such as poor bone formation, blindness and damage to the immune system.

HOW MUCH ENERGY DO WE NEED?

We all need different amounts of food to keep ourselves healthy. A gram of carbohydrate provides about 17 kJ of energy; a gram of fat about 38 kJ; and a gram of protein about 20 kJ. Most of our energy requirements in a balanced diet should come from carbohydrates.

The amount of energy that you need depends on three factors:

▶ The energy that you need to perform basic functions, such as breathing and maintaining body temperature. This is called the **basal metabolic rate** (BMR). It is on average about 7,000 kJ per day.

▶ The amount of exercise or activity that you do. A physical activity, such as running, can raise the BMR rate to 12,000 kJ a day.

▶ The amount of food that you eat – eating uses up energy during the digestive process.

When these three factors are put together it is possible to calculate an average daily energy requirement. Remember that these are only average recommendations – everyone is different.

As we get older, our energy requirements increase to a maximum in adulthood. This is because our basal metabolic rate needs more energy to support growth and development, and we need more energy to digest the larger food portions that we eat. If you are physically active you will need more energy to fuel your movements. Pregnant women also require a little more energy to feed their growing child. In later life we need less energy. This is because elderly people tend to be less active and their muscles become slightly smaller.

▲ You need to eat more if you are physically active.

AVERAGE DAILY ENERGY REQUIREMENTS

	Male	Female
8-year-old	8,500 kJ/day	8,500 kJ/day
Teenager	12,500 kJ/day	9,500 kJ/day
Office worker	11,000 kJ/day	9,800 kJ/day
Physical worker	15,000 kJ/day	12,500 kJ/day
Pregnant woman		10,000 kJ/day

INVESTIGATE

▶ Write a list of all the foods you have eaten in the last 24 hours and estimate the amounts of each. Look at the food labels and make an estimate of how much energy in kJ you have consumed. Does this match the recommended energy levels for your age group and gender?

OBESITY

With so many food types readily available in the western world, overeating has become a serious problem. Weight gain is also increasing because we are exercising less – transport and 'arm-chair' entertainment have become a way of life and snacks are available at every turn. Our lives are a far cry from those of our ancestors, who had to hunt for their food!

If you eat more than your body needs over a significant period of time, this extra energy is converted into fat and stored in tissues around the body. When the level of fatty deposits increases to a certain limit, a person is described as obese. Body fat is measured using a scale called body mass index (BMI) that divides your weight by your height. The BMI scale considers a person's weight and height so that different body shapes can be taken into account. Even so, a scale of this kind cannot be accurate in every case. For example, athletes with large muscles will have a larger BMI because muscle weighs more than fat.

HOW 'BIG' IS THE PROBLEM?

The problem of obesity is spreading. Approximately one in three US citizens (about six million people) are now obese and there are about 300 million obese people worldwide. Although the US and Europe are most commonly affected, newly developing nations such as China are quickly catching up. A significant proportion of the world's population are now risking their health through overeating.

HEALTH RISKS

Obesity can cause a whole range of health issues. If fat accumulates in blood vessels, the heart has to work harder to pump blood around the body and this may lead to heart failure (see page 37).

Obesity has also been linked to diabetes, a disease in which the body does not have enough insulin (a **hormone**) to control sugar levels in the body. Symptoms include frequent urination, excessive thirst, unusual weight loss and blurred vision. The disease can sometimes be fatal. Scientists have found that if a person accumulates excess fat and sugar in their bloodstream, the body's cells can become resistant to insulin. With so much extra fuel around, the cells begin to ignore signals to take more sugar from the blood. Over time, the body's cells may become permanently resistant to the effect of insulin.

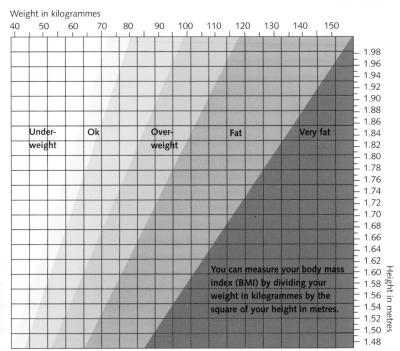

Weight in kilogrammes

Underweight | Ok | Overweight | Fat | Very fat

Height in metres

You can measure your body mass index (BMI) by dividing your weight in kilogrammes by the square of your height in metres.

◄ This type of graph is commonly used by doctors to indicate weight levels. A body mass index (BMI) of 20-25 is a healthy weight; a BMI greater than 25 is an indication of excess weight; and a value over 30 is considered to be obese.

CAUSES

Obesity occurs because people consume food containing more energy than they are able to use up. Modern lifestyles are a contributing factor – in the past, children played outside instead of watching television or playing computer games. Western populations also use extensive transport systems to get around. If physical activity is limited, the amount of energy that we 'burn off' is reduced. Fast food outlets that supply instant meals when you're on the go have also become a way of life for many people. These meals are usually high in saturated fats. Social class is thought to play a role in obesity, too. High fat foods are often cheaper than healthier alternatives – a tempting option for poorer families.

Sometimes, **genetics** plays a role in obesity. Studies are beginning to identify specific genes linked to obesity, although it is still not clear why some people can maintain a balance between the food they eat and the energy they use. Understanding more about the genetic causes of obesity may help to find new options for prevention and treatment. A tendency to store fat is believed to be the result of thousands of years of evolution in an environment where food sources were scarce. People who could store energy were more likely to survive periods of famine and to pass this gene onto their offspring.

▶ A combination of diet and exercise is the best way for people to lose weight.

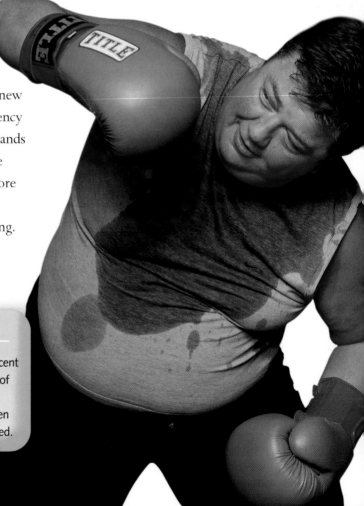

DID YOU KNOW?

▶ Babies born in the USA in 2000 have a 32 per cent chance (male) and a 38 per cent chance (female) of developing diabetes in their lifetime. This risk has been rising in the USA and similar trends have been seen in Europe. Changes in western diet are blamed.

SOLUTIONS

Although obesity may be a genetic condition in some cases, the disease can still be managed with lifestyle changes. A combination of diet and exercise is the most common method of losing weight. In more extreme cases, however, radical surgical procedures such as gastric bypass surgery are used – a procedure that closes off most of the stomach so that patients can no longer eat large quantities of food. Any kind of surgery brings risks but gastric bypass surgery is a popular option for many people who are desperate to lose weight.

Governments are becoming more aware of the obesity 'epidemic' engulfing the western world. Food labelling is now becoming a common requirement and public health campaigns are encouraging healthier lifestyle options.

Anorexia

Although obesity is fast becoming the latest epidemic of the modern western world, another equally serious (but quite different) weight problem is suffered by a small group of people. This condition is an eating disorder called **anorexia nervosa** (or 'anorexia' for short).

According to ideal weight guides, a BMI of less than 20 is considered to be underweight. However, a BMI of less than 16 is much more serious and indicates that a person is suffering from anorexia. People with anorexia diet intensely in search of an unrealistic body mass and shape. The condition is most common in women between the ages of 15 and 25, but men can also be affected. In western cultures, advertisements on television and in magazines often portray a slim figure as the 'norm'. Young women may see thin models as a role model and take weight loss to the extreme.

People with anorexia can lose weight in many different ways. Dieting, excessive exercise, vomiting and sometimes the use of **laxatives** ensure that the body quickly uses up any food that has been eaten. Anorexia is largely a psychological disorder and sufferers may be very secretive about their condition. Psychological therapy may be needed to encourage a patient to eat more (or in some cases, force-feeding may be necessary if the condition has become serious).

◄ Slim models in western society encourage young girls to aspire to an unrealistic body shape.

Dangers

Extreme weight loss can cause a number of health risks. Muscles grow smaller if the body begins to burn muscle tissue for energy (see page 13). This in turn causes tiredness and a general feeling of exhaustion. If your **immune system** becomes weak you are less likely to fight infections. Excessive weight loss can also interrupt a woman's menstrual cycle and may affect fertility. The body's chemical balance can also change, leading to deficiency diseases, heart failure and possibly death.

Bulimia

Bulimia is an eating disorder that is related to anorexia. Instead of starving their body, bulimics eat large quantities of food in a short time (known as 'bingeing') and try to prevent any weight gain by dieting, vomiting, exercising or using laxatives.

Did you know?

▶ Anorexia is common in particular sports where body image is important – such as dancing, gymnastics and ice-skating. In 1994, Christy Henrich, a world-class American gymnast died from anorexia. Christy began intense dieting after being told that she needed to lose weight by a competition judge. She resorted to anorexia and bulimia as a way to control her weight and the eating disorder eventually took her life. When Christy died, at the age of 22, she weighed less than 20 kilogrammes.

The digestive system

Once you have eaten your food, the process of digestion breaks it down into smaller parts so that your body can absorb the goodness that it contains. Digestion is both a mechanical and a chemical process. The body uses special chemicals to break food down into more manageable parts. Physical processes like chewing or mixing food also help to disintegrate the food that we eat. A number of different body parts are used in this complicated process.

Digestion begins in the mouth where, as you chew your food, your lips, teeth, tongue and saliva help to turn large, dry pieces of food into small, soft lumps that can be easily swallowed. Saliva contains an enzyme called 'amylase' that encourages the chemical breakdown of food. Amylase works mainly on carbohydrates. Your tongue is also covered in taste buds to help you to enjoy your food and to taste when food has gone bad.

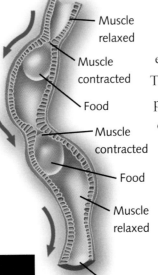

Muscle relaxed
Muscle contracted
Food
Muscle contracted
Food
Muscle relaxed

Oesophagus

OESOPHAGUS

When food has been chewed it enters the oesophagus (food pipe). The muscular walls of the oesophagus push your food along in a process called **peristalsis** – rather like squeezing toothpaste out of a tube. The action of swallowing also triggers the epiglottis (a piece of cartilage hanging at the back of the throat) to close over the trachea (wind pipe). This prevents food from going down the wrong way and causing you to choke.

STOMACH

The stomach can hold up to 1.5 litres of food and drink. Some of the food is dissolved by stomach acid and the stomach muscles help to mix food and enzymes together (an action called churning). A small ring of muscle around the top of the stomach opens to allow food to pass through and prevents stomach acid from reaching other body tissues where it could cause damage. The stomach also contains two other chemicals: a thick substance, called mucus, prevents stomach acid from damaging the stomach lining; and an enzyme, called pepsin, begins the digestion of proteins.

◄ Your mouth is the first part of the digestive process.

THE SMALL INTESTINE

Once your food has churned in the stomach for a couple of hours, it passes into the duodenum (the first part of the small intestine). Bacteria in the intestines help to break down your food and produce certain enzymes to speed up the process. Two important liquids are also added – pancreas juice and bile. Pancreas juice is made and secreted by the pancreas and contains enzymes that break down carbohydrates, proteins and fats. Bile is a yellowish liquid made in the liver and secreted by the gall bladder. It contains chemicals that neutralise the harmful stomach acid, enabling enzymes to work. Bile also helps to break down large pieces of fat so the enzymes can work more effectively. Your food then enters the jejunum and ileum where your digested food passes through the intestine lining so that your blood can carry the goodness to wherever it is needed in the body (see page 24).

Over 400 different types of bacteria live in your digestive system to keep it healthy. These 'good' and 'bad' bacteria usually live in harmony but if the balance changes you can become unwell with sickness or diarrhoea. Antibiotics are used to treat bacterial infections of the stomach. However, they also kill the good bacteria, too. Eating foods that are full of good bacteria (like yoghurt and cottage cheese) can help to retain a healthy balance.

THE LARGE INTESTINE

The small intestine leads into the large intestine through the caecum and into the colon. By this time most of the nutrients from your food have been absorbed. The remaining fibre, dead cells, bacteria and water are pushed along the colon by peristalsis and, as water is absorbed, the undigested food forms a solid waste called faeces. This waste is stored in the rectum and passes out of the body through the anus when you visit the toilet.

PARTS OF THE DIGESTIVE SYSTEM

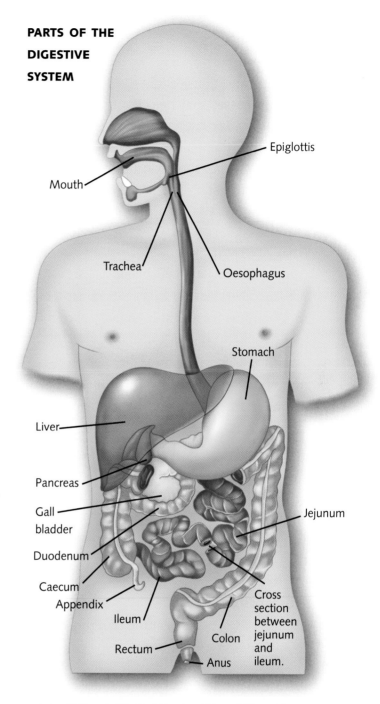

Epiglottis
Mouth
Trachea
Oesophagus
Stomach
Liver
Pancreas
Gall bladder
Duodenum
Caecum
Appendix
Ileum
Rectum
Colon
Anus
Jejunum
Cross section between jejunum and ileum.

DID YOU KNOW?

▶ The acid in your stomach is strong enough to burn rocks!
▶ Thanks to the process of peristalsis, astronauts can still swallow their food when they are upside down.
▶ The tubes of your digestive system would measure about nine metres if they were uncoiled and stretched out.

Enzymes

Chemical and physical changes are happening all the time in your body. It's these processes that help your cells to build new tissues, convert your food into energy and dispose of waste materials. The reactions that take place are speeded up thanks to special chemicals called 'enzymes'. Enzymes are essential for digesting food but they are also used in other body processes, such as stimulating the brain and repairing cells, tissues and organs.

WHAT ARE ENZYMES?

Enzymes are proteins found in our cells that speed up cellular reactions. They are essential to living creatures because without them, chemical reactions within our cells would occur too slowly to sustain life. Respiration and digestion are two processes that rely heavily on the action of enzymes. Enzymes help to break our food into the size and kinds of substances that our body can absorb and then help our body to release energy from this food. We need this energy to keep on the move and for our cells to carry out vital processes. If any one of the 2,000 enzymes in our body fails to work properly it can cause a serious illness.

PROPERTIES OF ENZYMES

Enzymes behave in different ways but they have five main properties in common:

1) Enzymes are reactive

Enzymes are described as working like a 'lock and key' – with the enzyme as the lock and the substrate (the substance it is working on) as the key. For an enzyme to work on a substrate, the two must fit together. They join at what is called the 'active site'. However, because the fit is slightly imperfect, the enzyme puts the substrate under strain. This encourages a reaction that speeds up the chemical process.

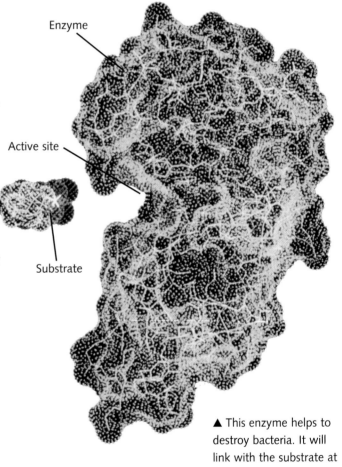

Enzyme

Active site

Substrate

▲ This enzyme helps to destroy bacteria. It will link with the substrate at the active site.

2) Enzymes are specific

Enzymes come in different shapes and sizes. Most enzymes will only react with a small group of chemical compounds while others will only work with one particular substrate with which they have a very close fit – just like Cinderella and her slipper.

3) Enzymes do not appear to be used up

When the substrate and enzyme lock together, a reaction occurs which changes the substrate into a different substance called the product. The product breaks away from the enzyme and the enzyme can be used over and over again.

4) Enzymes act at certain temperatures

Enzymes and substrates move around faster as they get warmer which increases their activity. However, above 40 °C, the specific shape of an enzyme is destroyed beyond repair and the substrate can no longer fit into the active site. The enzyme changes (becomes '**denatured**'), like boiling an egg, and this change cannot be reversed.

5) Enzymes act in certain acidity levels

Some enzymes like acidic conditions, such as the acid levels in your stomach, whilst others prefer neutral conditions. If an enzyme is subjected to a level of acidity that it doesn't like, it will not work effectively (or work at all).

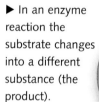
▶ In an enzyme reaction the substrate changes into a different substance (the product).

Enzyme   Substrate   Product

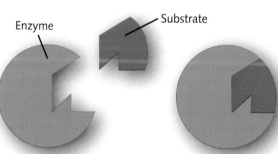
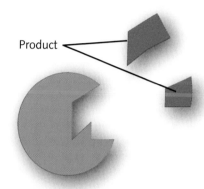

DID YOU KNOW?

▶ During a fever our body temperature can rise from 37°C up to 40°C. This can be very dangerous because our enzymes can become denatured (changed permanently) and no longer function. If we are cooled again, and not too many enzymes have been denatured, we can survive on those that are still functioning before our body replaces the enzymes we have lost.

▶ Some microscopic organisms, called 'extremophiles', can survive in extreme environments, such as acid hot springs or the scorching temperatures of volcano vents. These organisms can survive in acidic conditions, or when temperatures exceed 100°C, because their enzymes have adapted to suit such extreme environments. The discovery of extremophiles has greatly expanded the areas of Earth now considered to be habitable for life.

Although enzymes have very specific properties, their uses are widespread. Enzymes are essential for chemical reactions within our cells. They are particularly prominent in the digestive system, but also carry out processes like stimulating our brain, relaxing and contracting our muscles and eliminating carbon dioxide from our lungs. Enzymes also have a wide variety of uses in industry. As long as enzymes are used at the temperature and acidic levels that suit them, the results will not be disappointing.

MEDICAL DRESSINGS

One of the fastest acting enzymes in our body is called 'catalase'. This enzyme speeds up the breakdown of hydrogen peroxide, a chemical produced naturally by our cells. Catalase quickly changes hydrogen peroxide into oxygen and water, because in its natural state, hydrogen peroxide can damage or even destroy our cells. Because catalase works so quickly, we are not even aware that our bodies have produced hydrogen peroxide. The medical industry has used our knowledge of catalase to improve the effectiveness of medical dressings. Introducing hydrogen peroxide into the pad of a medical dressing encourages catalase from the wound to react with the hydrogen peroxide, producing oxygen. Oxygen speeds up the healing process and prevents harmful bacteria (that do not like oxygen) from entering the wound.

CLINICAL TESTING STICKS

Clinical testing sticks are used to test for the presence of biological molecules in our urine. This saves the expense of more complicated blood tests and can give a more direct result. Clinical testing sticks are used to test for diabetes and pregnancy, amongst other things. Enzymes contained within the tips of these testing sticks pick up specific molecules through the lock and key mechanism. The testing stick changes colour if a biological molecule is present and the enzymes are activated.

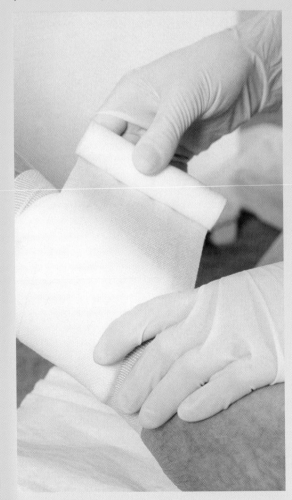
▲ Natural enzymes work with some medical dressings.

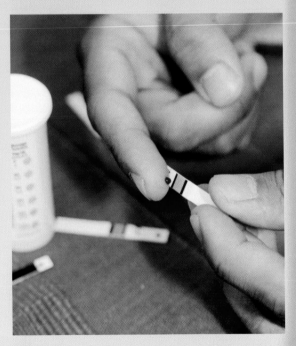
▲ Diabetics test their blood glucose levels regularly.

BIOLOGICAL WASHING POWDERS

Many everyday stains on our clothes – like sweat, blood and food – contain protein molecules. Biological washing powders contain enzymes called proteases, which break down proteins and help to remove these stains. To avoid protease enzymes becoming denatured, biological washing powders need to be effective at low temperatures. However, detergent manufacturers are now looking at the enzymes found in extremophiles that are well adapted to high temperatures. If these enzymes can be extracted and studied, in the future we may be able to make our own enzymes that work at higher temperatures.

▲ Enzymes help to get your clothes really clean.

THE TEXTILE INDUSTRY

Leather is a material taken from the hide of cattle. Untreated leather is a hard material and difficult to wear. Manufacturers make leather softer by adding protease enzymes that remove proteins in the material.

THE FOOD INDUSTRY

Enzymes have a number of roles in the food industry, including the manufacturing of bread, cheese and alcohol. Enzymes can also improve the consistency of the food that we eat.

UNUSUAL USES OF ENZYMES IN THE FOOD INDUSTRY

Use	Purpose
Meat preparation	Enzymes tenderise the meat to make it more tasty
Slimming products	Enzymes convert sugar into a sweeter product that is less fattening
Chocolate	Enzymes are added to liquid chocolate to allow it to flow more easily before it sets
Fruit juice	Enzymes are added to make the juice look less cloudy
Ice cream	Enzymes are added to make ice cream smooth because it has a tendency to be lumpy

6

Absorbing food

Digestion is of no use unless our food can be absorbed into the body. The small intestine is specially designed to absorb the food that has been digested. Here, carbohydrates, proteins and fats are processed and distributed to the parts of the body where they are needed most. Some nutrients are used as building blocks to grow and repair the cells. Others are converted to energy so that the body can move and maintain a healthy temperature.

HOW DOES ABSORPTION OCCUR?

The small intestine is lined with thousands of tiny folds, called villi. Each villus contains a network of blood vessels that absorb the nutrients from runny, digested food. The tiny villi are only one millimetre long, but together they form a surface that is 20 times the area of the skin! This means that as many nutrients can be absorbed as possible. The villi are only one cell thick so food passes through them easily. Villi also have a blood vessel that transfers the food directly to the blood to be transported around the body. Fats cannot be absorbed into the blood, but villi have a 'lacteal vessel' that transports fat to the **lymphatic system** where it is digested.

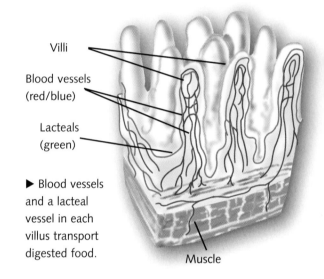

Villi

Blood vessels (red/blue)

Lacteals (green)

▶ Blood vessels and a lacteal vessel in each villus transport digested food.

Muscle

▲ This coloured electron scan shows the villi (orange) and micro-villi (red) that line the small intestine. Magnification approximately x 100.

THE DRIVING FORCES

When your food is squeezed along the ileum, pressure pushes it into the villi. Some digested food is absorbed through the process of **diffusion** (where varying pressure on the surface of a cell encourages substances to move into and out of the cell).

WHAT IS ABSORBED?

Digested carbohydrates and proteins are taken into the blood where they are transported directly to the liver for sorting. The liver helps to filter, store and prepare these nutrients. If too many carbohydrates are consumed, the excess is turned to fat and deposited around the body. Proteins from food can also be changed into specific proteins that the body needs. Proteins from the liver are transported to make new tissues to heal a wound, for example. Excess proteins are excreted in the urine.

DID YOU KNOW?

▶ Alcohol can be absorbed directly through the stomach wall. People can feel drunk quite quickly because alcohol bypasses most of the digestive system.

GETTING RID OF WASTE

The human body is designed to get rid of waste products that might be harmful to us. Some obvious examples include the action of coughing and sneezing as well as sweating and breathing out carbon dioxide. When it comes to the digestive system, the body has a series of specialised organs that help to filter and expel waste materials. Undigested food in the large intestine forms a solid waste called faeces. This waste is stored in the rectum. The faeces then pass out of the body through the anus.

WATER CONTROL

The main purpose of the large intestine is to absorb the water from food so the body does not become **dehydrated**. If you are ill with diarrhoea, this absorption is less effective and the body loses a lot of water in the faeces. This can be dangerous if left untreated because the body starts to 'dry up' and cells can't function properly. If you put your hands on your hips, your thumbs will be pointing to the approximate position of your kidneys, near your back (see below).

Water from undigested food passes into the blood where it is taken to the kidneys through the renal artery. Inside each kidney, there are thousands of small tubes called nephrons. As the blood travels near the nephrons, it is under high pressure as it passes from the wide renal artery to narrower blood capillaries – just like a crowd of people walking down a wide corridor and then trying to pass though a narrow door. This high pressure filters your blood because many substances are squeezed out, including important salts, a waste product called 'urea' and excess water. The nephrons are surrounded by blood vessels and as the waste substances pass through them, the kidneys reabsorbs some of the salts and water, passing them straight back into the blood via the renal vein.

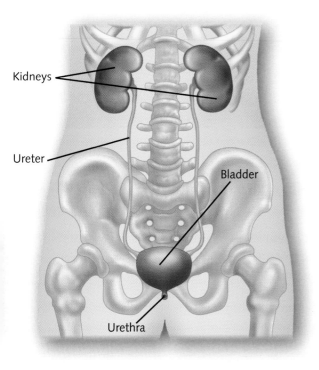

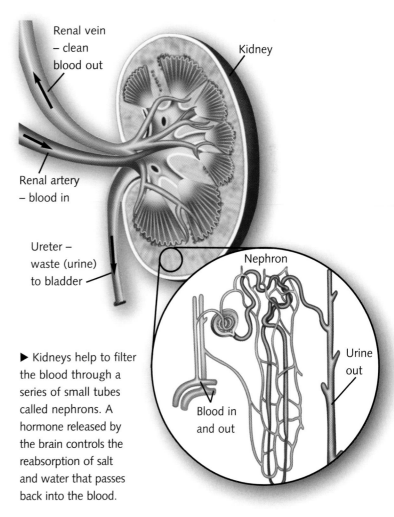

▶ Kidneys help to filter the blood through a series of small tubes called nephrons. A hormone released by the brain controls the reabsorption of salt and water that passes back into the blood.

PASSING FLUIDS

The fluid that remains in the nephron passes to the ureter and then to the bladder via the urethra. This is the urine that you pass at regular intervals when you go to the toilet. If you drink a lot of water your urine will be pale and dilute because this water has not been reabsorbed back into the blood. However, if you are dehydrated your urine will be darker in colour because it is more concentrated.

HOW MUCH WATER SHOULD WE DRINK?

Your body is two-thirds water and this level must be maintained to keep you healthy. Many parts of the body contain water, including the brain, blood and lean muscle. Every day you lose about two litres of water as you sweat, breathe and go to the toilet. You replace this water by drinking liquids and eating food.

If you are thirsty it is your body's way of telling you that it needs more water. You lose more water in hot weather and when you exercise so it is particularly important to replace fluids at these times. If you become dehydrated, you may feel thirsty and also suffer from headaches. Dehydration is not just a lack of water, but also of important salts such as sodium and potassium that are essential for the healthy functioning of the nerve cells.

▲ It is important to drink more water when you exercise.

DID YOU KNOW?

▶ Athletes who consume large quantities of water during exercise can risk consuming too much water. If this happens, the blood increases in volume and important salts become diluted. If salts are also lost through sweating a low blood salt level may result. This can lead to a lack of functioning of the brain, heart and muscle tissues. This condition is called hyponatremia and early symptoms include fatigue, apathy and nausea. Hyponatremia is often confused with dehydration, but drinking more water can be fatal. Recreational drugs, like ecstasy, have also been known to cause hyponatremia. Ecstasy users can feel thirsty and drink more water than their body needs. They are advised to sip water rather than drink it in large amounts.

Some people find that their kidneys do not function properly because they have been damaged or affected by disease. Although you can survive with just one kidney, if both kidneys fail to function, urgent treatment is needed. Excess water, salts and urea need to be removed from the body to prevent damage to cells that may eventually lead to death.

KIDNEY DIALYSIS

In the short term, people with failing kidneys can be treated using a kidney dialysis machine. This takes the role of a kidney by filtering the blood and removing waste products, before returning the blood back to the patient. A dialysis machine needs to be used for approximately five hours, two or three times a week. Sometimes patients have a kidney dialysis machine in their home; but many need to visit a hospital for treatment. This can have a huge impact on the patient's quality of life as regular treatments are needed. Kidney dialysis patients must be careful to avoid salty foods, such as crisps and crackers, which would otherwise alter the balance of water and salt in their blood and cause further illness.

KIDNEY TRANSPLANTS

Replacing a diseased kidney with a donated kidney can be a cure for many people with kidney failure. However, many patients have to wait a long time before a suitable donor becomes available. Kidney transplants can also be complicated because:

▶ A donated kidney must be a good match in terms of tissue type. A patient's immune system can often react to and reject a new kidney.

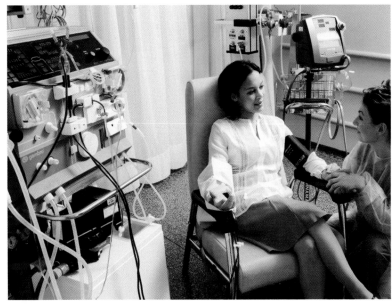

▲ A kidney dialysis machine is used to filter the blood of patients who have kidney failure.

▶ Sometimes, relatives of the patient donate a kidney because they offer the best tissue match. However, this is not always the case.

▶ Some kidney donations come from patients who are being kept alive on a life support machine but who have no chance of recovering from their illness or injuries. It can be difficult for relatives to decide whether their loved ones should have important organs removed for transplantation surgery. In the UK, many people carry donor cards, or have registered online, to say that in the event of their sudden death, they would like their organs to be donated for others to use.

Patients who have had transplantation surgery are given medication to suppress their immune systems as a precaution. Unfortunately this means that they may contract an infection and become ill. Patients need to be kept in sterile conditions for some time after the operation until their immune system becomes stronger, but some kidney transplants still fail nevertheless.

▶ New treatments are being developed all the time that, in the future, may improve the lives of patients whose kidneys have become damaged or diseased.

XENOTRANSPLANTATION

Xenotransplantation is the transplantation of organs across species. The technique had some degree of success when it was first used in 1984 to give a newborn baby a baboon heart – the baby lived for about 20 days. In the future, pigs may be used for xenotransplantation because they have organs that are similar in size to human organs and pigs reproduce quickly. It may also be possible to produce cloned pigs that have genetically-altered organs that are suitable for human use. However, more recent studies have shown that xenotransplantation may not be as safe as previously thought. Some animal organs have been found to transfer viruses that could be harmful to humans.

STEM CELL RESEARCH

Stem cells are cells that have not developed into a specialised cell type. They are found in early **embryos** (although scientists have also recently found them in adult bone and skin tissues). Every cell in your body 'stems' (originates) from this type of cell. Scientists have been looking at how stem cells can be used to restore tissues that have been damaged by injury or disease. Transplanting stem cells into damaged kidneys, for example, might encourage the stem cells to

specialise and grow new, healthy kidney tissue. However, although it is quite straightforward to grow kidney tissue, the kidney itself is made up of different cells and tissue types that form a particular structure. To grow a new organ from stem cells would be very difficult. The long-term side effects of stem cell transplantation are also as yet unknown.

TISSUE ENGINEERING

Tissue engineering is a technique developed by two American doctors, Joseph Vacanti and Bob Langer, in 1987. Instead of using stem cells, the technique uses tissue taken from a body that has been donated to medical science. The tissue is grown on specially shaped 'scaffolding' so that it adopts the shape that is required (for example, an ear). To date, scientists have been able to use this technique to grow skin for burn victims. However, in the future it may become possible to grow more complicated tissues like cardiac muscle, muscle tissue and even organs such as kidneys.

▶ **Dr Joseph Vacanti and his colleague Bob Langer pioneered the development of tissue engineering.**

OTHER DIGESTIVE PROBLEMS

▶ Irritable bowel syndrome (IBS) is a disease in which the large intestine fails to work properly. Symptoms include cramping, diarrhoea and constipation. Some people with IBS find that certain foods (such as alcohol and dairy products) trigger their symptoms. There is currently no cure for the condition but medication and diet can alleviate symptoms.

▶ Crohn's disease is a condition that usually affects the small and large intestines. Symptoms include diarrhoea, pain, weight loss and fatigue.

The cause is unknown and there is, as yet, no cure. Treatments try to relieve symptoms. Sometimes, part of the intestine needs to be removed to control the condition.

▶ A number of diseases can affect the liver causing tiredness, weight loss, sickness and diarrhoea. However, because the cells of the liver are able to regenerate themselves, a diseased liver can sometimes return to normal function. Drinking too much alcohol can cause a liver disease called cirrhosis. This is a serious condition because the effects are sometimes irreversible.

Moving things around

7

Some small animals are able to rely on the process of diffusion to move nutrients and waste products between their cells. However, larger creatures, like humans, need a more complicated system (called the 'circulatory system') to transport food, oxygen and vital nutrients around the body. The circulatory system is the body's lifeline and is composed of the blood, blood vessels and heart.

CIRCULATORY SYSTEM

The circulatory system carries nutrients to our cells and removes waste material. The system is also used to regulate body temperature and other levels, such as the amount of sugar and water circulating around the body, to keep it healthy. The heart is the driving force behind the movement of blood, which travels through blood vessels called arteries, capillaries and veins.

THE HEART

The heart lies between the lungs, at the front of the chest, and slightly to the left. Arteries carry blood away from the heart to all of the major organs of the body. Veins carry blood from the organs back to the heart. The heart is made of two pumps that power a separate blood cycle.

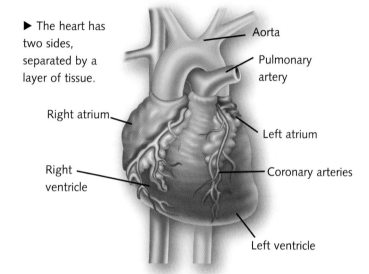

▶ The heart has two sides, separated by a layer of tissue.

Aorta

Pulmonary artery

Right atrium

Left atrium

Right ventricle

Coronary arteries

Left ventricle

The right side pumps blood to the lungs to collect oxygen and back again. The left side pumps **oxygenated** blood to the rest of the body. Once this is done, **deoxygenated** blood returns to the heart and the cycle begins again. Blood passes through the heart twice for each complete circuit of the body which takes about a minute.

ACTION OF THE HEART

When the heart beats, both sides beat together but they are completely separated by a layer of tissue. The blood contained in the two sides cannot mix together, which makes our circulatory system work more efficiently. Some babies are born with a 'hole in the heart' – a hole in the tissue separating the two sides which blood can pass through. This makes the heartbeat less efficient, so doctors try to repair the hole using simple surgery.

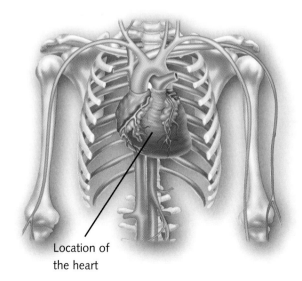

Location of the heart

The heart has four chambers. The chambers on the top are called atria and those on the bottom are called ventricles. Blood fills up both sides of the heart from the atria, through to the ventricles. When the ventricles are full, valves between the upper and lower chambers close, the heart beats and blood is expelled under high pressure through the appropriate arteries. It is important for the valves to close so that the blood does not pass back out through the atria when the heart beats. The heartbeat is caused by an electrical impulse that the cardiac muscle of the heart generates on its own.

LEAVING THE HEART

Arteries carry oxygenated blood away from the heart (the only exception is the pulmonary artery, which carries deoxygenated blood from the heart to the lungs). When the heart beats, it does so with an enormous force to ensure that all the blood is expelled and delivered to places as far away as the toes. The blood in the arteries is under very high pressure so the artery walls are very thick and muscular. The artery will expand slightly and then

contract as the blood passes through. This also helps to push the blood along. As arteries carry blood at a high pressure, we would bleed to death very quickly if we cut an artery. This is why arteries are located deep within our skin and are difficult to see. Sometimes, arteries must pass over other structures, such as bones in the wrist or tubes in the neck. When this happens it is possible for us to feel the heartbeat as a pulse. The average adult pulse is 70 beats per minute.

▲ You can feel your heartbeat as a pulse in your wrist.

ENTERING TISSUES

Arteries lead into capillaries, which are very thin vessels found in the tissues of our organs. It is here that oxygen and nutrients pass into our body cells (to be replaced by waste products). Capillaries are found in capillary 'beds' that feed a group of cells. Capillaries are very thin which makes it easy for substances to move into and out of them. When blood flows into the capillaries it is moving under high pressure and is therefore squeezed out through the capillary bed. This has the effect of pushing oxygen and nutrients into the cells, reducing the level of blood pressure. These substances also pass into our cells by the process of diffusion (see page 24). The blood leaving the capillary bed now contains waste materials.

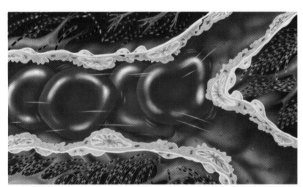

▲ Illustrated red blood cells flowing through a capillary at high pressure. Magnification approximately x 5,000.

GOING BACK TO THE HEART

The blood is at a low pressure when it enters the veins which are situated near the top of our skin and are usually located in muscle tissue. When we expand or contract our muscles as we move about, the blood is squeezed upwards and eventually

makes its way back to the heart. The blood is now at a lower pressure and generally travelling against gravity. However, veins contain valves, which prevent your blood from flowing backwards. These valves are situated at regular intervals and as the blood flows upwards they close, catching any blood that might fall down.

VEIN VALVES

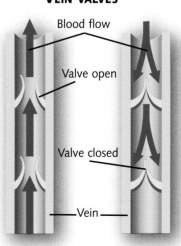

Blood flow

Valve open

Valve closed

Vein

Blood components

The blood is made up of billions of cells, all floating in a watery liquid called plasma. Adults have about five litres of blood in their bodies. Children have about half this amount, but grow more blood cells as they get older.

The liquid part of blood is called plasma. Plasma is mostly made up of water, but there are many other substances dissolved within it. These include sugars and vitamins, urea, hormones and **antibodies** that help our immune system.

The 'red' part of blood is made up from three different types of blood cell – red blood cells, white blood cells and platelets. A tiny drop of blood the size of a pinhead contains 5 million red blood cells, 15,000 white blood cells and 250,000 platelets. Each cell type has a different role to play in the working of the body. Blood cells don't last forever. When they die they are broken down by the liver and expelled from the body as waste products. Red blood cells live for about four months and platelets for just one or two weeks. White blood cells may last for just half a day or longer than a year, depending on the type.

Red blood cells

Red blood cells look like little doughnuts. They are responsible for carrying oxygen from the lungs, and energy-rich sugars, vitamins and nutrients from food, to the cells around the body. Red blood cells contain a substance called haemoglobin. Oxygen attaches itself to the haemoglobin so that it can be transported around the body. Haemoglobin also transports a substance called nitric oxide that helps with the control of blood pressure, for example by making blood vessels wider when you exercise to transport more oxygen to your cells.

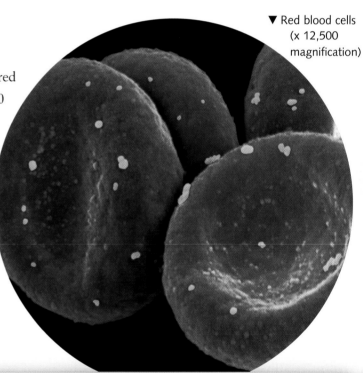

▼ Red blood cells (x 12,500 magnification)

Time Travel: Into the future

▶ Casualties of serious accidents often need blood transfusions to replace the blood that they have lost. If blood is not replaced quickly, organs can become deprived of oxygen and damaged. Ambulance crews don't carry blood to the scene of an accident – blood types need to be carefully matched to an individual and samples can be wasted because they don't last very long. Instead, ambulance crews carry a saline solution that boosts the amount of fluid in a patient's blood as a temporary measure until they reach hospital. In America, doctors have just started using a synthetic compound that can act as artificial blood in the place of saline. The product, made by a company in Illinois, is called PolyHeme and contains haemoglobin extracted from human blood. PolyHeme can carry oxygen for seriously injured casualties until a blood transfusion can be given. This artificial blood can help to save time, and ultimately save lives.

WHITE BLOOD CELLS

White blood cells have a white appearance. They help to fight infection and are an important part of the immune system. White blood cells engulf harmful bacteria and viruses and disable or destroy them. There are two types of white blood cells that help to fight disease — phagocytes and lymphocytes.

▲ Lymphocyte (x 7,000 magnification)

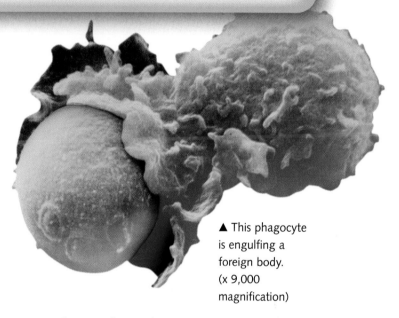

▲ This phagocyte is engulfing a foreign body. (x 9,000 magnification)

Phagocytes fight disease by engulfing foreign bodies that appear in the blood. Phagocytes have a lobed nucleus that helps the cell to grow around a foreign body and engulf it. Once engulfed, the cells release an enzyme, which essentially digests the foreign body.

Lymphocytes have a large round nucleus that produces substances called antibodies. Antibodies have a complicated role, but help to fight bacteria in the body. Lymphocytes collect in the lymph nodes when we have an infection and this causes the lymph nodes to swell. Sometimes, when you are unwell you can feel this swelling in your neck.

PLATELETS

Platelets are fragments of cells that help with the clotting process. When we cut ourselves, platelets that are exposed to the air trigger a series of chemical reactions that result in a blood clot being formed. Clotting blood helps to heal cuts on the skin or damage inside the body.

We now know that blood circulates around the body through a network of arteries, veins and capillaries. But at one time, scientists were at a loss as to how the blood travelled and how it transported oxygen and nutrients around the body. Thanks to the work of two prominent doctors – Galen and Harvey, working 1,500 years apart – the mystery began to be unravelled.

GALEN'S THEORY

▲ Claudius Galen

Claudius Galen was a Greek doctor living during Roman times (129-216 BCE). Anatomy was difficult to study at this time because the Church objected to human dissection (and the Church's influence was very strong). However, Galen expanded his knowledge of the human body by dissecting animals and comparing his findings.

Galen believed that there were two types of blood: venous blood (which we now called deoxygenated blood) and arterial blood (which we now call oxygenated blood). He thought that these two types of blood had different roles relating to the three main parts of the body: the liver, the heart and the brain.

For Galen, venous blood came from the liver and provided nourishment and growth, while arterial blood came from the heart to provide vitality to other body parts. Today, we know that blood is recirculated around the body, but Galen thought that venous and arterial blood were used up. He also believed that the heart sucked blood in as it filled up (rather than acting as a pump as we now know) and that blood pushed itself through the blood vessels unaided.

Galen's theory that there were two distinct types of blood failed to explain properly how the arterial blood came to contain oxygen. Galen believed that arterial blood seeped through hidden holes in the tissue separating the two sides of the heart where it mixed with venous blood. Instead of blood passing through the lungs to pick up oxygen (as we now know) Galen thought that the blood 'mingled' with air in the lungs and a special vessel called the pulmonary vein contained air that mixed with blood in the heart.

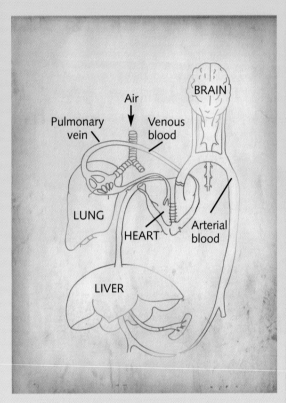

▲ A diagram showing Galen's view of the way in which blood circulates around the body.

Galen's theory, although far from perfect, was generally well received for nearly 1,500 years. Until the 1600s, no alternative explanation of blood circulation was given.

WILLIAM HARVEY'S THEORY

William Harvey was a British physician who lived during the 1600s. Harvey studied at Cambridge University as well as at Padua in Italy where his experiences put him at the forefront of medicine. Although Galen's theories were still strong at that time, Harvey began to look much more closely at the blood system by dissecting animals (most famously the King's deer because Harvey was a royal doctor). Harvey's studies confirmed that the heart worked as a muscle – the ventricles contracted to expel blood and the arteries pulsated because of the shockwave from the beating of the heart.

Harvey initially published his ideas by pointing out the flaws in Galen's theory. He looked for air in the pulmonary vein, but found only blood there. He then discovered that the heart is the centre of a circulatory system. By studying frogs, Harvey showed that the amount of blood that left the heart in a minute could not conceivably be absorbed by the body and continually replaced by blood made in the liver. In fact, Harvey noticed that the amount of blood forced out of the heart in an hour far exceeded the volume of blood in the frog. This showed that the blood must constantly move in a circuit, otherwise the arteries and body would explode under the pressure.

▲ William Harvey

Harvey failed to display the complete circuit through which the blood flows but he came very close to understanding the circular movement of the blood. Harvey couldn't see the tiny connections that linked the capillaries to the veins, but he used a simple experiment to reveal that these connections must exist. First, Harvey tied some material tightly around the forearm so that no arterial blood could flow. The veins in the lower arm were normal but soon became swollen. When the tie was loosened slightly the arterial blood flowed down, but the venous blood could not flow back again. This showed that when the materal was tight, blood had poured down the arteries and then back up the arm within the veins. Harvey's experiment showed that there was an undiscovered pathway in which blood travelled from the arteries to the veins. This new understanding had very little effect on the practice of medicine in Harvey's lifetime, but was to become the foundation for modern research into the heart and circulatory system.

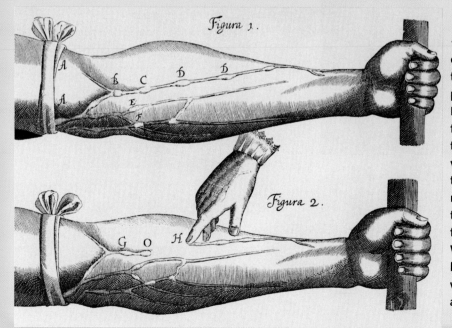

Figura 1.

Figura 2.

◄ This illustration shows one of the experiments that William Harvey published in 1628. Here, Harvey shows that blood from the arteries is linked to the veins and that the veins flow only towards the heart. When the material on the forearm is tight (figure 1), the veins fill and become swollen. When the material is loosened (figure 2), the veins become less visible as the blood flows again.

Nowadays, people live much longer than they used to. At one time the average lifespan was 40 years, but many people now live to more than twice this age thanks to improved healthcare and more favourable environmental conditions. However, as we grow older, some circulatory diseases become more common.

HYPERTENSION (HIGH BLOOD PRESSURE)

The strength at which the heart pumps blood around the body is called blood pressure. Blood pressure should be kept within a healthy range. If your blood pressure gets too low, you can feel faint because less blood (with oxygen) reaches the brain. High blood pressure is a condition that generally affects older people as the muscular walls of the arteries become less supple and the smaller blood vessels get narrower.

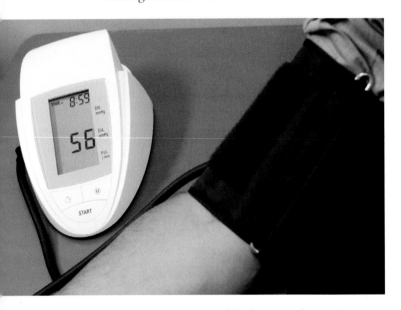

▲ Doctors measure your blood pressure by putting a blood pressure cuff around your arm, inflating the cuff and listening for the flow of blood.

Constant high blood pressure can put unnecessary strain on the heart and cause it to work hard. People with high blood pressure are more likely to suffer a heart attack or a stroke (where a blood vessel in the brain bursts or get

blocked, starving surrounding cells of oxygen). Stroke patients may lose some functioning of their brains and may need to relearn basic tasks such as speaking and walking.

High blood pressure can also be caused by:
▶ Stress
▶ Being overweight
▶ Smoking and drinking
▶ Lack of exercise
▶ Poor diet (including too much salt)
▶ Genetic factors

People with high blood pressure are advised to change their lifestyle to keep their blood pressure at a safer level. Some people are given medication to bring their blood pressure down. Cutting down on fatty food, not smoking and exercising regularly all help to lower the risk.

You may have felt your heart rate increasing when you are scared. Fear or excitement causes the adrenal glands above the kidneys to release a hormone called adrenalin into the blood. This chemical speeds up the heart rate to provide the muscles with extra energy and oxygen, in case you need to fight or run away. If you live a healthy lifestyle this increase in heart rate and blood pressure is not dangerous because your heart is used to coping with sudden changes of heart rate.

ARTERIOSCLEROSIS

Arteriosclerosis is also a disease of the circulatory system. If we eat lots of fatty foods, our blood vessels can become clogged with fatty deposits. This can restrict the flow of blood to important organs of the body, which become deprived of the oxygen they need to work properly.

The cardiac muscle of the heart has many arteries serving it to make sure it receives an adequate supply of oxygen. A painful condition called angina occurs when a narrowed artery restricts the flow of blood to the heart. If a narrowed artery is completely blocked by a blood clot, a painful seizure called a heart attack can occur. A heart attack means that part or all of the heart muscle stops working and can be fatal if not treated promptly, because other organs are soon deprived of vital oxygen.

Arteriosclerosis and heart attacks can be caused by:
► A high-fat diet
► Obesity
► Lack of exercise
► Smoking
► Genetic factors

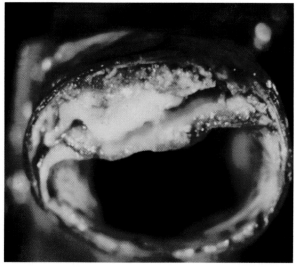
▲ Blood cannot flow well through this narrowed artery.

THE BENEFITS OF EXERCISE AND A GOOD DIET

A low-fat diet prevents fatty deposits from building up in the blood vessels. Saturated fats are the worst culprits because they can be deposited quickly. These fats come from animals (such as those found in meat and dairy products) and are commonly used in processed food. Saturated fats cause the body to make more cholesterol and other fats that don't dissolve in the blood.

Exercise is good for the circulatory system. It helps to burn excess calories that would otherwise cause weight gain. When you exercise your muscles need more oxygen, energy and nutrients than when you are at rest. Exercise temporarily increases the heart rate and blood pressure and the arteries widen to allow blood to flow more freely. This improves the circulation and ensures that the blood vessels are working well.

▲ Exercising regularly is a good way to keep a healthy heart.

Exercising for at least 15 minutes, three times a week, will keep your heart in good condition. Your resting blood pressure will fall and a healthy heart is able to cope with a little extra strain if needed. Studies also show that exercise gives us a sense of wellbeing — if we are more relaxed we are less likely to put unnecessary strain on our hearts.

Holding it all together

Our bodies are a system of working organs that keep us healthy and alive. But without a skeleton, you would be a soggy heap on the ground! Your skeleton protects your organs, supports the tissues of your body and allows you to move.

THE FRAMEWORK

When a skeleton is found inside the body it is called an 'endoskeleton'. Some animals, such as crabs and shellfish, have their skeleton on the outside (an 'exoskeleton'). This is useful for protecting the soft parts of their body but can make movement restricted.

▲ This crab has its shell on the outside.

The human skeleton is made up of over 200 bones that link together to form a structure that is light, strong and flexible. Over half of the bones are found in the wrists, hands, feet and ankles. Living bones aren't dry and brittle (like the bones you see in museums) but are tough and flexible and they grow as we get older. The bones are supplied with blood vessels, and nerves that sense pain.

The skeleton has the following functions:
▶ **Support** – humans are able to stand upright due to the strength of their skeletons. The bones that hold us together support the shape we adopt.
▶ **Protection** – vital organs and tissues are protected from damage by the bones of the skeleton. For example, the ribs protect the heart and lungs and the skull protects the brain.

▶ **Movement** – our skeletons are designed to offer flexibility that enables us to move. We have joints that allow bones to move independently of each other. Bones attach to muscles that pull on our bones, making us move.
▶ **Storage** – bones are an important storage for calcium and other minerals.
▶ **Manufacture of blood cells** – the **bone marrow** inside our bones constantly manufactures new red blood cells.

▲ Your skeleton has joints that enable you to move and to use your limbs to carry out different skills.

The skeleton is made up of three main parts:

▶ **Axis** – the central column, which includes the skull, spine and ribcage. The spine (or backbone) is actually a series of 33 very small bones called the vertebrae. These small bones give us the flexibility that we need to move about each day.

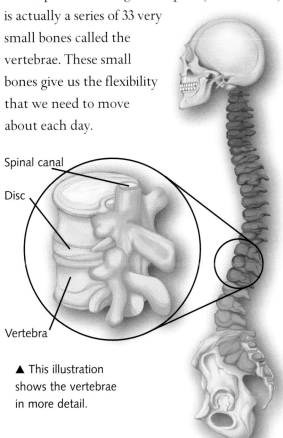

▲ This illustration shows the vertebrae in more detail.

Spinal canal
Disc
Vertebra

The ribcage is important for protecting all of the soft organs found beneath it. This includes the heart and lungs. Organs that are not protected by the skeleton (such as the kidneys) are more susceptible to damage.

▶ **Appendages** – these include all the limb bones. The arms and legs follow the same basic pattern – both have larger bones connecting them to the main frame of the body. Beneath the elbow joint there are two bones in the arm (the ulna and radius) enabling a twisting of the lower arm. In the leg there are also two lower bones – the tibia and fibula. The long bones in the arms and legs are wider at the ends than in the middle, which makes them light and strong.

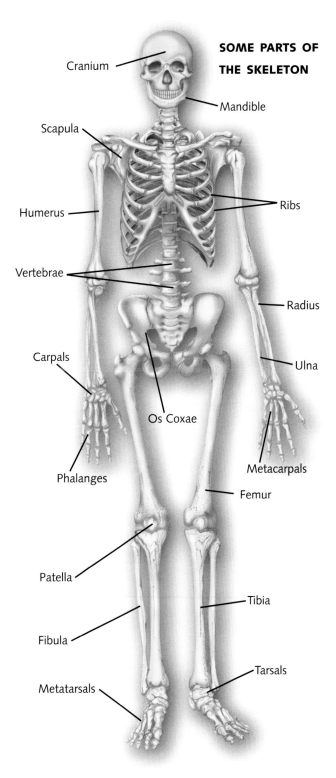

SOME PARTS OF THE SKELETON

Cranium
Mandible
Scapula
Humerus
Vertebrae
Ribs
Radius
Ulna
Carpals
Os Coxae
Phalanges
Metacarpals
Femur
Patella
Tibia
Fibula
Metatarsals
Tarsals

▶ **Girdles** – the girdles connect the bones of the appendages to the bones of the axis. They are the bones of the pelvis and the bones of the shoulders, including the collarbone and shoulder blades.

WHERE BONES MEET

Where two bones meet we have what is called a 'joint'. Joints allow our bones to move freely. There are a number of different types of joints:

▶ Hinge joints

Hinge joints are found in the fingers, knees and elbows. They allow movement in one direction only, like the hinges of a door. Pieces of tissue, called **ligaments**, hold the bones in a fixed position that only allow them to move in one direction.

▶ Ball and socket joints

Ball and socket joints are found in the hips and shoulders and allow us to move these parts in all directions. The end of one bone forms a ball that fits tightly into the end of the other bone (called the socket). The bones are also held together with ligaments, but much more movement is permitted.

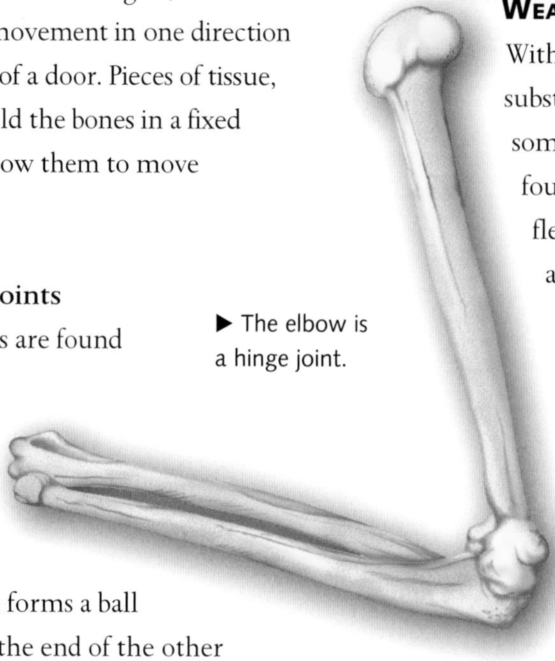

▶ The elbow is a hinge joint.

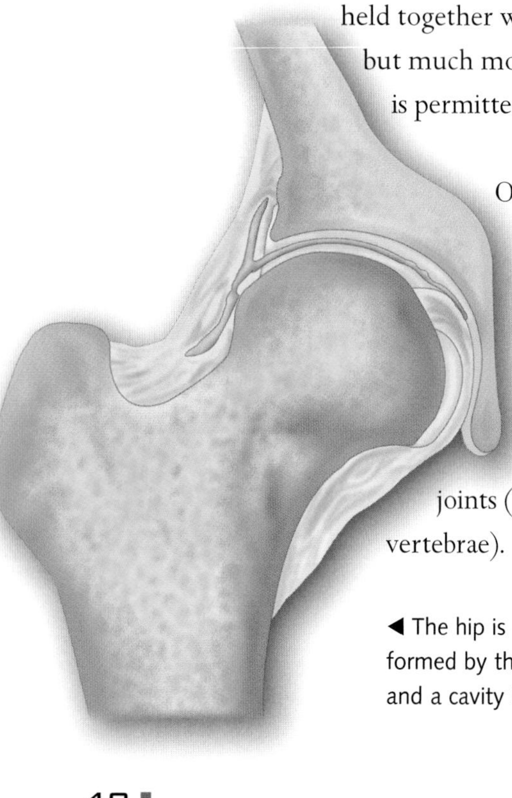

Other types of joint include pivot joints (e.g. the neck), fixed joints (e.g. the skull and pelvis) and gliding joints (e.g. the vertebrae).

◀ The hip is a ball and socket joint formed by the head of the femur and a cavity in the hip bone.

TEST YOURSELF

▶ By looking at a model of the human skeleton, find each of the joint types described below and note the amount and direction of movement each one allows.

WEAR AND TEAR

Within the skeleton is a rubbery, gristly substance, called **cartilage**, which holds some bones together. Cartilage is also found in parts of the body where more flexibility is needed (such as the elbows and the knees). Cartilage helps to reduce wear and tear when these bones rub together. Some parts of the body, such as the nose and outer ear, are also made from cartilage.

Bones that constantly move and rub against each other would quickly become worn if the joints were not well designed. Hinge and ball and socket joints are also called 'synovial joints'. They are sealed units and contain a fluid (synovial fluid) that reduces friction as the two bones move. The ends of the bones are also covered in cartilage that acts as a shock absorber during movement. Synovial joints are mainly in your limbs where movement is important.

TIME TRAVEL: INTO THE FUTURE

▶ Scientists have found a new way to treat broken bones that allows them to heal faster. The treatment involves a paste that is injected directly in the fracture and resembles bone material once it hardens. The paste has greatly reduced the need for plaster casts and screws to hold bones together as they heal.

MUSCLE POWER

Although our skeletons are the frameworks on which our bodies are built, we could not move around without muscles. Muscles give the body strength, help us to move around and keep our heart and other body parts moving.

There are approximately 350 muscles in the human body which make up about two-fifths of our body weight. Muscles are found from the face and limbs to inner organs such as the heart, stomach and lungs. You can control the movement of most of your muscles (called skeletal muscles), but others (called smooth muscles) work automatically inside the body.

Skeletal muscles are attached to two bones and as they work, they cause bones to move towards or away from each other. When you bend your knees, for example, muscles attached to the bones above and below the knee do all the work. Muscles also help you to perform smaller movements, such as blinking or raising an eyebrow. Your brain sends a signal to your skeletal muscles when you want to move.

DID YOU KNOW?

▶ Smiling uses about 20 facial muscles, while frowning uses over 40.
▶ Two dentists recently found an unidentified muscle in the skull when they began dissecting the skull from a different angle to traditional dissection methods. The muscle is on average four centimetres long and stretches from the eye to the lower jaw.

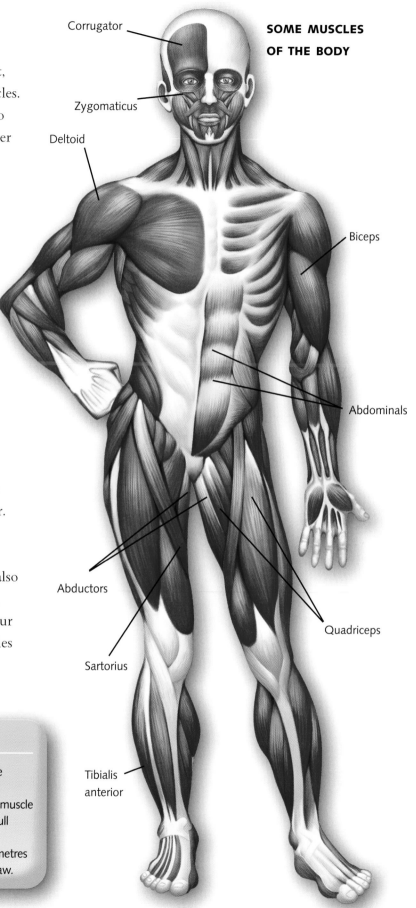

SOME MUSCLES OF THE BODY

Corrugator
Zygomaticus
Deltoid
Biceps
Abdominals
Abductors
Quadriceps
Sartorius
Tibialis anterior

How do muscles work?

Muscles are able to relax and contract because they are made of fibres that slide over each other. These fibres are bound together in a series of bundles. The end of the bundle is called a **tendon** and tendons are the parts of the muscle that attach themselves to the bones. Tendons should not be confused with ligaments (which hold bones together at joints so they do not drift apart).

When muscles contract, they shorten and the bones to which they are attached are forced to move. Muscles can pull on bones but they can't push against them. Instead,

they act in pairs, one on each side of a bone. The muscle pair works as a team – one muscle pulls the bone one way and then relaxes, while the other muscle pulls it back again. For example, when we raise our arm, the biceps muscle contracts and the triceps muscle relaxes. When we lower our arm again, the reverse is true.

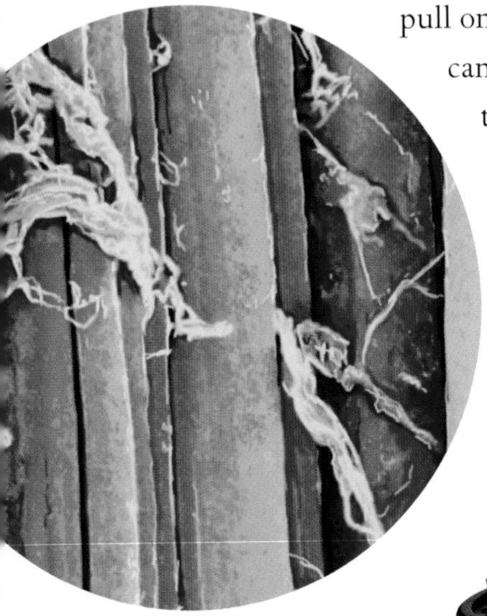

▶ Extended arm

▼ Flexed arm

Biceps Triceps

Biceps Triceps

▲ Muscle fibres are about the thickness of a hair.

INVESTIGATE

▶ Look at a piece of raw steak and try to see the groups of fibres. Separate out these fibres by putting the piece of steak into some salt solution. If you have a microscope, examine the pieces under the lens. What can you see?

▶ Ask a friend to hold a ruler up in the air and then release the ruler for you to catch it. Make a note of the reading on the ruler where you catch it. Repeat five times and switch places with your friend. Who has the fastest reaction time?

TEST YOURSELF

▶ When an athlete begins to run a race, what are the muscles of the leg doing, as the athlete is in the blocks and as they begin to run?

▶ Which of these movements use skeletal muscles and which use smooth muscles?

(1) A hair growing

(2) Swallowing

(3) Walking

DIFFERENT MUSCLES

There are three main types of muscles.

▶ **Voluntary muscles** – these skeletal muscles are attached to the bones so you can move them whenever you want to (when you lift your arm, for example). Voluntary muscles can contract and relax quickly, but they soon become tired.

▶ **Involuntary muscles** – these smooth muscles contract and relax automatically in the body. You cannot control the action of these muscles but they carry out some very vital processes. For example, the muscles of the intestines contract and relax to push our food along. Involuntary muscles contract and relax slowly so they do not become tired, like skeletal muscles. Other involuntary muscles include the lining of the hair follicles, the lining of the blood vessels, the stomach muscles that churn our food and the muscles that move urine from the kidneys to the bladder.

▶ **Cardiac muscle** – this is a special type of muscle found only in the heart. It contracts and relaxes about seventy times per minute. The cardiac muscle is an involuntary muscle that works automatically.

REFLEXES

In times of danger we can move very fast – we have sharp senses and our voluntary muscles are quick to respond. Sometimes however, we can act without thinking. This is called a reflex. If we touch something hot, we often move our hand before our brain recognises the pain. Similarly, we can move to catch a falling object before we have even thought to catch it! Reflexes help us to act very quickly, particularly if we are in danger. They are useful in many sports, too.

▲ Having good reflexes is useful when playing ball sports, such as basketball.

Like all body parts, bones and muscles can become damaged or diseased. This can cause problems with mobility and strength. Thanks to advances in medical science however, many common problems can now be treated effectively.

A PROBLEM WITH MUSCLES

Muscular dystrophy is an inherited disease which mainly affects boys. The disease causes the muscles to become weak and wasted. Symptoms usually start when a child begins walking – the child may start to walk at a later age than is usual or they may find that they frequently fall over. The symptoms don't become fully obvious until about the age of three, however, when the child will have difficulty climbing stairs and getting up from the floor. Children with muscular dystrophy also tend to have large calf muscles and wasted muscles at the tops of their arms and legs. Although the condition is largely untreatable, physiotherapists work with muscular dystrophy patients to keep them mobile as long as possible.

A PROBLEM WITH JOINTS

Arthritis is a disorder that causes the joints to become swollen, painful, stiff and eventually deformed. Arthritis is brought on by a swelling of synovial joints and tends to affect the hands, ankles, hips and knees. Persistent swelling can damage the ends of the bones in the joint and the cartilage that covers and protects them. Arthritis is more common in older women.

There is no cure for arthritis. However, the condition can be treated with medication to reduce the swelling of the joints and to slow down any long-term damage. In some cases, where joints have been damaged beyond repair, a joint replacement may be offered.

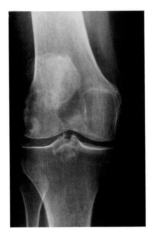 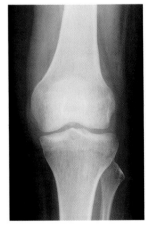

▲ This arthritic knee (left) is more inflamed than the healthy knee joint (right).

◀ This day centre is caring for children with muscular dystrophy.

JOINT REPLACEMENTS

Hip replacement surgery is becoming more and more common as the world's population ages. The hip joint is commonly replaced because a damaged hip has a significant effect on free and flexible movement and therefore quality of life. Hip replacements are made from metal, ceramic or plastic and are designed to fit onto the damaged bone in the ball and socket joint. Thanks to increasing medical advances, the quality of life of many people has improved with an artificial hip.

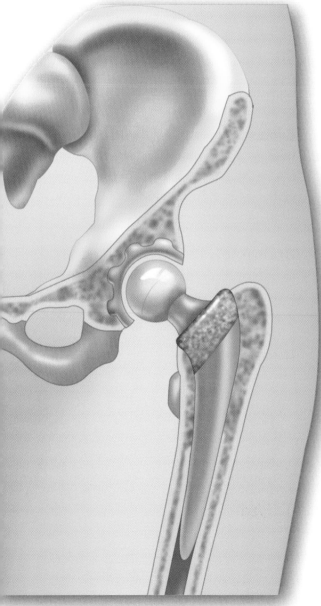

▲ Hip replacements are made from metal, ceramic or plastic.

A PROBLEM WITH BONES

Osteoporosis is the most common disease of the bones. Osteoporosis is a loss of bone tissue which weakens the bones, making them more likely to fracture and crumble. This reduces the strength and protection that bones give our body tissues. Osteoporosis occurs naturally in the elderly when bone tissue is made at a slower rate. Osteoporosis can also be accelerated in some women by the onset of the **menopause**. Many people do not know that they have the disease until they fracture a bone; usually the hip bone, which is under the most pressure. The following guidelines can help to prevent the onset of osteoporosis:

▶ **Eat a diet rich in calcium** – bone tissue is manufactured from calcium. Foods such as dairy products, beans and fish are sources of calcium.

▶ **Carry out weight-bearing exercise**, such as walking, jogging, aerobics and weight training – this strengthens your bones earlier in life so they can endure more as you get older.

▶ **Do not smoke and limit your intake of alcohol** – the effects of smoking and alcohol increase the chance of osteoporosis in later life.

▶ **Hormone replacement therapy** – some older women, who have passed through the menopause, are advised to take hormone replacement therapy to keep their bones strong.

TIME TRAVEL: DISCOVERIES OF THE PAST

▶ Ancient Egyptians are thought to have given us the first replacement body parts (prosthetics). Archaeologists have recently found a mummy of a women in her fifties that has a prosthetic toe. Her original toe had probably been amputated and the prosthetic toe was carved from wood and attached by leather strings.

Glossary

ANOREXIA NERVOSA – An eating disorder whereby a person starves themselves or tries to lose weight by other means so that they become dangerously thin. Anorexia nervosa is largely a psychological condition.

ANTIBODIES – Proteins in the blood that are produced by the immune system to destroy or weaken dangerous substances that could harm the body.

BASAL METABOLIC RATE – The rate at which energy is used by an organism at rest.

BLOOD PRESSURE – The pressure exerted by the blood against the walls of the blood vessels, particularly the arteries. Blood pressure varies with the strength of the heartbeat, the volume and thickness of the blood, the elasticity of the blood vessels and a person's age and general health.

BONE MARROW – The fatty tissue that fills some bones. Bone marrow is the main source of red blood cells, platelets and most white blood cells. Bone marrow releases up to 15 million new red blood cells every second.

BULIMIA – An eating disorder whereby a person binges and then tries to prevent weight gain (for example, by dieting or vomiting) so that they become dangerously thin. Like anorexia nervosa, bulimia is largely a psychological condition.

CALORIE – A unit of energy-producing potential that a source of food contains. A calorie is equal to the amount of energy required to raise the temperature of one gram of water by 1°C.

CARDIOLOGIST – A doctor who studies the structure and function of the heart and the circulatory system.

CARTILAGE – A tough, elastic tissue found in areas of the body, such as the joints, the nose and the ear. Cartilage helps to hold some of your bones together.

CELL – The smallest unit of an organism that is capable of functioning on its own. The human body contains over 200 cell types.

CHOLESTEROL – A fatty substance found in animal tissue and various foods. Cholesterol is an important feature of cell membranes but too much cholesterol in the blood can lead to heart disease and other circulatory conditions.

DEHYDRATION – An excessive loss of water from the body. Dehydration can be caused by an illness or by a lack of fluids. When a person becomes dehydrated, important salts are also lost from the body.

DENATURED – When a substance changes irreversibly. An egg is denatured when it is cooked.

ANSWERS

p11 Test yourself
Example answers: Carbohydrates – the primary source of energy for all body functions; eating too many carbohydrates can lead to weight gain; eating too few carbohydrates can lead to low energy levels. Proteins – help to maintain and replace the tissues in the body; eating too many proteins can lead to weight gain; eating too few proteins can limit healthy growth and development. Fats – the body's major energy storage system and also used to protect organs and bones, to make hormones and to regulate blood pressure; eating too many fats can lead to weight gain and health problems such as heart disease, obesity and diabetes; eating too few fats can lead to weight loss, muscle loss and low energy levels. Vitamins and minerals – important substances that help the body to work effectively and to grow and develop; eating too many vitamins and minerals can cause an imbalance of chemicals in the body; eating too few vitamins and minerals can lead to a range of deficiency diseases.

p26 Test yourself
(1) Bladder
(2) Kidneys
(3) Renal artery
(4) Urethra

p30 Test yourself
Order of statements – 2, 5, 1, 3, 6, 4.
Ventricles have to pump blood all the way around the body.

DEOXYGENATED – To have dissolved oxygen removed (from the blood, for example).

DIFFUSION – The spontaneous movement of substances from an area of low concentration to an area of high concentration (or vice versa).

EMBRYO – An organism in its early stages of development.

ENZYMES – Proteins produced by living organisms that help to speed up chemical reactions.

GENETICS – The scientific study of heredity.

HORMONES – Chemical messengers produced by glands in the body. Hormones are transported by the blood to other organs to stimulate their function.

IMMUNE SYSTEM – A system of organs, tissues, cells and substances that protect the body against disease and infection.

LAXATIVE – A food or drug that stimulates the action of the intestines to remove waste from the body.

LIGAMENT – A tough, fibrous tissue that fastens bones or cartilage together at a joint.

LYMPHATIC SYSTEM – A network of vessels, carrying lymph, a tissue-cleansing fluid, from the tissues into the veins of the circulatory system.

MALNUTRITION – Poor nutrition which may be caused by a limited diet or by an illness.

MENOPAUSE – A natural occurrence in older women, when the menstrual cycle permanently stops.

NUTRIENT – Any substance that is nourishing or provides food for a living organism.

OBESITY – Increased body weight caused by an excessive accumulation of fat.

OXYGENATED – To be combined with oxygen.

PERISTALSIS – The wave-like muscle contractions that move food through the digestive system.

RESPIRATION – The process of releasing energy from food.

TENDON – The long, stringy cords that attach muscles to bones.

TOXIN – A poisonous substance produced by living cells, which can cause harm to the body.

Useful websites:
www.bbc.co.uk/schools
www.nationalgeographic.com
www.sciencenewsforkids.org
www.newscientist.com
www.howstuffworks.com

---

p33 Test yourself
Red blood cells – carry oxygen, sugars, vitamins and nutrients to cells around the body.
White blood cells – help to fight infection and are an important part of the immune system. There are two main types of white blood cells: phagocytes engulf foreign bodies that appear in the blood and lymphocytes produce antibodies.
Platelets – help the blood to clot so that a wound heals when you cut yourself.

p40 Test yourself
Example answers: Hinge joints – fingers, knees, elbows. Hinge joints allow movement in one direction only. Ball and socket joints – hips, shoulders. Ball and socket joints allow movement in all directions. Pivot joints – neck, the joint between the radius and ulna in the forearm. Pivot joints allow a rotating movement. Fixed joints – skull, pelvis. Fixed joints allow no movement. Gliding joints – vertebrae, fingers, toes. Gliding joints allow a limited amount of movement.

p43 Test yourself
On the blocks: thigh contracted (shortened) and hamstring, calf and shin muscles relaxed.
On the off: thigh muscle contracts to straighten the knee as it leaves the block, calf muscle contracts to straighten the ankle.

(1) A hair growing (smooth muscles)
(2) Swallowing (smooth muscles)
(3) Walking (skeletal muscles)

Index

Page references in italics represent pictures.

Thrilling Quilling

THE ULTIMATE QUILLER'S SOURCEBOOK

Elizabeth Moad

David and Charles

www.mycraftivity.com

A DAVID & CHARLES BOOK
Copyright © David & Charles Limited 2008

David & Charles is an F+W Publications Inc.
company
4700 East Galbraith Road
Cincinnati, OH 45236

First published in the UK in 2008

Text and designs copyright © Elizabeth Moad 2008
Photography and illustrations copyright © David
and Charles 2008

A catalogue record for this book is available from
the British Library.

ISBN-13: 978-0-7153-2854-5 hardback
ISBN-10: 0-7153-2854-9 hardback

ISBN-13: 978-0-7153-2851-4 paperback
ISBN-10: 0-7153-2851-4 paperback

Printed in China by SNP Leefung
for David & Charles
Brunel House, Newton Abbot, Devon

Commissioning Editor: Jane Trollope
Assistant Editor: Emily Rae
Project Editor: Jo Richardson
Designer: Eleanor Stafford
Production Controller: Ros Napper
Photographers: Karl Adamson and Kim Sayer

Visit our website at www.davidandcharles.co.uk

David & Charles books are available from all
good bookshops; alternatively you can contact
our Orderline on 0870 9908222 or write to us
at FREEPOST EX2 110, D&C Direct, Newton
Abbot, TQ12 4ZZ (no stamp required UK only);
US customers call 800-289-0963 and Canadian
customers call 800-840-5220.

Contents

Introduction

Quilling is the papercraft that started me off on my creative career ten years ago, and is the craft that I have since been drawn back to over and over again. The technique of quilling is a particular skill and yet it is easy to do. By simply turning a basic tool and thereby manipulating strips of paper, wonderful shapes and forms can be created that have numerous decorative applications. This explains why it has always appealed to me and is increasingly growing in popularity. In addition, quilling requires very little equipment and materials, so it can be carried out anywhere using just the manual quilling tool, glue and paper. This makes it a very economical craft too, with packets of ready-cut paper strips purpose designed for quilling being inexpensive and allowing plenty of scope for trial and error without undue expense. The only investment is your time and this is often what daunts the beginner. But time is a relative concept and also doesn't mean complication, so in this book I have set out to dispel the myth that quilling is necessarily a long and involved process. Here, I have presented a wide variety of quilled elements and motifs that are individually quick to make, which can then be used in combination to construct larger projects.

Quilling is also a craft that can bring much satisfaction and joy to the creator. The act of twirling, curling and coiling the strips of paper is very relaxing and therapeutic in times of stress. What's more, it is an authentic craft in a world of quick-fix consumerism and ready-to-assemble kit crafts. Most importantly, it brings a lot of happiness to those who receive a quilled card or gift – and money just can't buy that!

History

Paper quilling, or 'paper filigree' as it is sometimes called, has a history that can be traced back over 500 years. The exact origins are not known, as paper degrades over time, but it is thought that the first quillers were members of religious institutions creating paper art for devotional purposes. However, examples of quilling do exist that date from Georgian and Victorian times, when ladies of leisure decorated tea caddies and boxes with rolled paper shapes – a craft thought appropriate for gentlewomen of the time. These ladies rolled papers around the quills of bird feathers, which is how the craft gained its name.

Having caught on in England in the late 18th and early 19th centuries, quilling spread to the American colonies. It subsequently experienced a decline, only to resurface in the 21st century with a flourish to become a popular modern craft that is now practised throughout the world.

Elizabeth

How to use this book

If you are a beginner in this craft, it is a good idea to start by familiarizing yourself with the papers (see pages 6–7) and basic equipment (see pages 8–9) needed for quilling. The coils and pinched-coil shapes displayed on pages 12–15 are the most frequently used forms in quilling, and although this is not an exhaustive guide, it is best to practise with these to begin with. For the novice quiller, it is worthwhile spending some time initially just experimenting with paper strips – coiling, curling and pinching them – to become acquainted with how the techniques work in practice.

This book is specially structured so that you can dip into any themed chapter that suits your mood or purpose, from Flower Power to Party Time, and choose any project that appeals, rather than having to follow it from start to finish. And each project includes a comprehensive 'you will need' list and clear step-by-step instructions, accompanied by a gallery of inspirational ideas on how to use and apply your quilled decorations and designs in a variety of creative ways.

Papers

Quilling is all about the paper, given that it is entirely formed from strips of paper. Traditionally, quillers would cut their own strips from paper sheets, but today most quillers purchase pre-cut strips to the width they require in the colours they want. The quiet satisfaction of opening a new packet of papers that has arrived through the mail is one that is treasured and shared throughout the quilling fraternity!

Weights

The weight of paper used for quilling is crucial, as it determines the end result. Paper about 100gsm in weight is best. This weight is strong enough to coil easily and holds its shape. Paper that is too thin will be flimsy and crease, but if it is too thick, it won't coil or make flowing coils.

Widths

Pre-cut paper strips come in several standard widths, but many suppliers will trim paper to the width you require. The following widths are used in this book:

- 1.5 or 2mm (¹/₁₆in) – the minimum width that is available
- 3mm (¹/₈in) – the most common width and ideal for beginners
- 5mm (³/₁₆in) – good for freestanding 3-D quilling work
- 10mm (³/₈in) – the most common width for use with a fringing tool
- 15mm (⁵/₈in) – some suppliers offer this width for making frilly flowers (see page 115), with the adjustable 90 degree-angled fringing tool (see page 9)

Colours

The papers come in every shade imaginable, so the beginner may find selection a daunting process, or an expensive one if they fail to make the right choice. It is therefore advisable at first to buy a packet of pink, yellow or green shades or a 'rainbow' pack with a basic range of colours, to give you just enough to choose from. As you find colours that you like, you can then buy a whole pack of just one colour to extend your stock.

Single colour

Packs of ready-cut strips of paper are available in a single colour and the colour extends all the way through the paper.

Single colour with metallic edge

Gilded with a metallic edge, this paper looks fantastic when it catches the light. It is available in copper, gold and silver. You can also buy papers edged with metallic red, green, blue or purple. These are ideal for Christmas motifs and themes (see pages 106–113), and for creating light-catching butterflies (see Fluttering Butterfly, page 37), as well as for adding alluring sparkle to your quilling work in general.

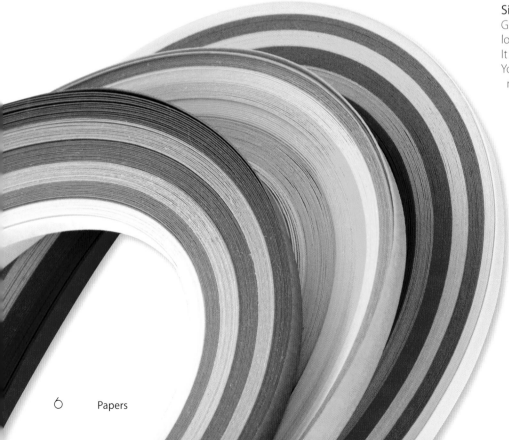

Different colour on either side

These papers are generally used for the Spreuer technique (see page 17).

Graduated colours

Paper strips can be graduated in colour along their length, for example ranging from pale at one end to darker in the centre and pale again at the other end. Other papers graduate in colour across their width. These can be used to create highly attractive frilly flowers (see Frilled to Thrill, page 115) and hat trimmings (see Tendril-trimmed Hat, page 76).

Cutting your own

It is possible to cut your own strips of paper by hand, but this can be time-consuming and also demands a high degree of precision, since the strips must be cut to exactly the same width. Some people use a paper shredder (not the cross-shredder type) to cut strips of paper for quilling. The advantage of professionally cut strips is that you can be sure of their uniformity and therefore will give an even finish every time.

Storage

Once you have accumulated paper strips, it is important to store them so that they are easily accessible and won't become crushed. Plastic storage units are readily available and inexpensive. These units come in many sizes and those that incorporate several drawers are best. You can then organize your papers into different colours, widths and special finishes to facilitate the selection process.

Equipment

The good news is that quilling doesn't require a huge array of tools. In fact, only one specialist item – a simple quilling tool – is needed. The following is a guide to the basic essentials and how to choose a quilling tool that's right for you.

Basic tool kit

Many of these items are general papercrafting tools and equipment, but some need specially selecting for quilling purposes or are specific to quilling.

Cutting mat, craft knife and metal ruler

A self-healing cutting mat is essential for cutting with a craft knife, and also protects your work surface. A craft knife should always be used with a metal ruler; those with a cork base prevent slippage.

HB pencil and eraser

Required for marking lines on graph paper and for tracing templates.

PVA (white) glue

Regular PVA (white) glue is fine, but it should not be too runny. Too much water in glue makes the papers overly wet. A tacky PVA is best, but you can use a water-based non-toxic glue as long as it dries clear.

Small, fine-pointed scissors

Vital for snipping and trimming the narrow strips of paper.

Small, fine-pointed scissors

Fine-tipped tweezers

These are invaluable for picking up and positioning coils, wiggly eyes, gem stones and other embellishments. The pair shown is self-locking, which avoids having to keep them squeezed.

Self-locking, fine-tipped tweezers

Quilling tools

These come in all shapes and sizes, but all consist of a two-pronged slot through which a paper strip is threaded. They can be very cheap, but even the most expensive is not much to pay for a lifetime's service. It is important to find the tool that suits you. Some people prefer long handles, while others favour shorter ones that fit into the palm of the hand. When choosing, check the size of the gap at the curling end. A large gap means a large hole in the centre of the coil, which is most noticeable when making tight closed coils. Two of the quilling tools shown below comprise a sewing needle with one end snipped off embedded into a wooden handle. These have a gap just wide enough to slot the paper through to create a very small central hole in a tight coil.

Fine-tip applicator or cocktail sticks (toothpicks)

Many quillers find a fine-tip applicator attached to a pot of glue the most precise way to apply glue direct to paper, as shown above. The pot is stored upside down in a jar on a damp sponge so that the glue doesn't dry in the nozzle. Alternatively, you can use a cocktail stick (toothpick) or needle tool (see right) to apply small dots of glue.

Other quilling methods

Some quillers prefer to make coils by rolling the paper around a needle tool (see below) or just using their fingers. The advantage of a quilling tool is that the slot catches the end of the paper so that you can make coils just by turning the tool, otherwise you need to actively wrap the narrow paper strip with your fingers. As I have always used a tool and find that it is much easier for beginners to use, this is the method featured throughout the book.

Needle tool

This metal point on a handle is useful for rolling paper around to leave a hole in the centre.

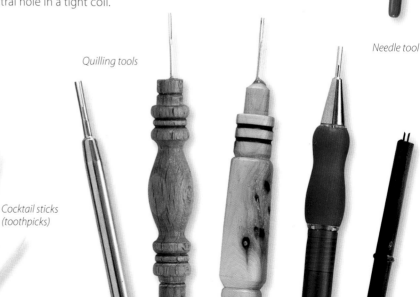
Quilling tools

Needle tool

Cocktail sticks (toothpicks)

Fringing tools

These enable you to fringe narrow paper strips with speed and precision for use in quilling (see page 16). By manually moving the handle of the fringing tool up and down, the paper strip is pulled through and sliced either 90 degrees across or at a 45 degree angle, leaving an uncut margin so that the paper remains in one piece.

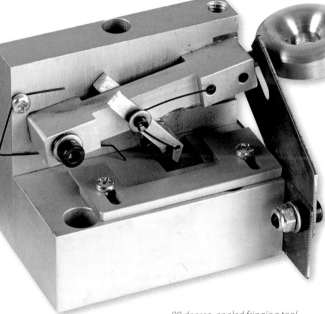

Adjustable 90 degree-angled fringing tool – for varying widths of paper up to 15mm (⁵/₈in) wide

90 degree-angled fringing tool – for papers 10mm (³/₈in) wide

45 degree-angled fringing tool – for 10mm (³/₈in) wide paper folded in half

Snips
Used in needlework, snips can be useful as an alternative to fringing tools for snipping or fringing paper, in preference to scissors, since they automatically release.

Bulldog clips
When manually fringing paper, you need a wide or very wide bulldog clip to hold the edge of the paper securely while you cut.

Bulldog clip

Snips

Further tools and materials

These tools have been used in the book for different effects and you may decide to purchase them once you have mastered the basics. Also included here is a representative selection of materials and embellishments used in the projects.

Board and pins
A thick piece of foam, polystyrene or Styrofoam board, used for the husking technique (see page 16), allows pins to be inserted to position and hold papers in place. A cork board can be used instead.

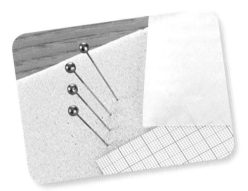

Magnifier
Very intricate work can be tiring on the eyes, so a magnifier should be used to avoid eyestrain.

Onion holder
This consists of a series of metal prongs on a plastic handle around and through which paper is looped to create intricate designs, known as the Spreuer technique (see page 17). Originally designed to slice onions, internationally renowned quiller Jane Jenkins found a better use for the holder and the quilling world forgot about the onions!

Ribbler (crimper)
By turning the handle of this tool, two cogs are turned and the paper is fed through and ribbled or crimped.

Onion holder

Wooden spoons or dowel
Many quillers keep lengths of wooden dowel around which to make large rings of paper (see Precious Rings, page 53). However, I lose mine, so I tend to use wooden spoon handles, as I know where these are! But any smooth, round object can be used for this purpose.

Quilling board
This cork- or foam-based template board has a plastic top with cutout circles of various sizes, into which you can insert coils and let them unwind to achieve the exact size of coil.

Ribbler (crimper)

Magnifier

Quilling board

Wooden spoon

Felt-tip pens and brush pens

Felt-tip pens are used to colour the ends of fringed paper strips, as in the Dainty Daisy, page 45, and finer brush pens to add features to quilled items, as in the Fairy Queen, page 60.

Chalks and applicator

Coloured chalks can be applied to coils, such as in the Fairy Queen, page 60, or to the edges of fringed papers.

Coloured chalks and applicator

Perfect Pearls™

This metallic powder is mixed with water and brushed onto coiled shapes to create a gilded finish – see the Fairy Queen Crown, page 59.

3-D paint

As its name implies, this paint has more volume than ordinary paint, so is ideal for adding three-dimensional details to quilled items, such as flower stamens – see Beautiful Bloom, page 72. Bear in mind that it does take a relatively long time (at least two hours) to dry.

Fancy-edged scissors

These scissors have blades with a decorative edge. They can be used to cut 10mm (³/₈in) wide paper for quilling, as in Dazzling Daffodil, page 43.

Fancy-edged scissors

Wiggly eyes

These eyes that move around are great for bringing quilled animals and other crazy creatures to life, such as the Staring Starfish, page 85, and Dotty Bug, page 34, adding an extra fun element to your designs. They are available in a variety of different sizes.

Punches

Small punched shapes can be attached to strips for coiling and forming flowers – see Beautiful Bloom, page 72.

Gem stones

Small gem stones can be added to coils for rings – see Precious Rings, page 53 – or for eyes – see Hovering Dragonfly, page 36. These are also perfect for highlighting flower centres.

Ribbon and bow-maker

A bow-maker comprises lengths of wooden dowel of different heights and diameters set in a block, and is very handy for making very tiny ribbon bows for quilling – see Polka-dot Bikini, page 86 – as well as perfectly symmetrical bows.

Adhesive foam pads

Available in a wide range of shapes and sizes, these can be used for mounting quilled motifs and embellishments onto card and other surfaces. The mini variety (2mm (¹/₁₆in) high) is ideal for mounting paper to the same height as the quilling (see Wedding Cake, page 52, and Spotty Buggy, page 56).

Wiggly eyes

Punches

Bow-maker

Gem stones

Adhesive foam pads

3-D paint

Basic techniques

The fundamental factors involved in quilling are: the length of paper used for coiling, how much the coil is allowed to unwind and whether or not the end of the coiled paper is glued in place. So here you can see how these factors are used in practice to produce different types of coil, and how the resulting coils can be manipulated to create various shapes.

How to make a coil

Insert a strip of paper into the slot of the quilling tool 2mm (¹/₁₆in) from the end of the paper strip. Here, a 3mm (¹/₈in) wide paper strip is used.

Turn the quilling tool to catch the end of the paper strip.

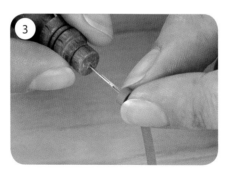

Continue to turn the tool. I always turn the tool away from me, but in workshops I have found that many people prefer to turn towards them; there is no hard and fast rule. Guide the coil with your fingers and keep a light tension on the paper with your spare hand.

Continue turning to the end of the strip of paper, then carefully remove the tool by sliding the paper off the prongs, holding the coil in place.

TIP
If you make a mistake, just discard the coil and try again – the cost is minimal.

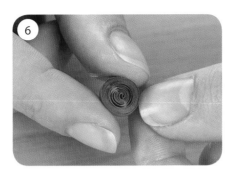
5

Add a dot of glue to the end of the paper strip with a cocktail stick (toothpick) or fine-tip applicator (see page 8) and adhere to the coil to create a tight closed coil.

6

Alternatively, release the coil a little and then glue the end of the strip to the coil to create a shape with thick edges – a loose closed coil.

7

If you release the coil further, it becomes larger in size.

8

Release the coil even further or let go altogether to create an open coil.

9

Alternatively, insert the coil into a template in a quilling board (see page 10) to achieve a specific size of coil.

TYPES OF COIL

Tight closed coil

Loose closed coil

Loose closed coil released further

Open coil

Pinching loose closed coils

Loose closed coils are where the end of the paper has been glued to the coil, but the coil has been allowed to unwind a little so that it becomes loose while remaining closed. The basic coil can then be pinched between the thumb and index finger at one or more points to form a variety of different shapes, as follows.

Teardrop – pinch at one point.

Bent teardrop – pinch at one point, then pull the point round to bend.

Eye (sometimes called a marquise) – pinch at two opposing points.

Triangle – pinch at three points an equal distance apart.

Square – pinch at two points, as for the eye above right, and at another equally spaced two points, then push two opposing pinched points in opposite directions to form a square.

Diamond – as for the square on the left, but stood on its tip.

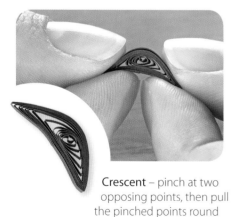

Crescent – pinch at two opposing points, then pull the pinched points round and inwards to bend.

TIP

You may find that some coils are too small to manipulate, in which case simply allow them to unwind a little more before gluing the end in place and pinching.

Bug-head crescent or half-circle – pinch at two points relatively close together, leaving the curve of the coil intact on the opposite side.

Star – pinch at four equally spaced points, then press inwards towards the centre at both opposing pinched points.

Heart – hold the coil in one hand and pinch at one point while simultaneously pushing inwards with a fingernail at the opposing point.

Rectangle – pinch at two opposing points, then pinch again at two opposing points a short distance from the first two pinched points.

Holly leaf – see steps 1–3, page 112.

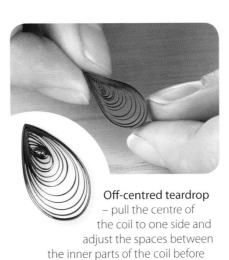

Off-centred teardrop – pull the centre of the coil to one side and adjust the spaces between the inner parts of the coil before pinching on that side.

OPEN COIL SCROLLS

For open coils, the quilling tool is removed and the coil is left to assume its shape without being glued at all. All kinds of scrolled decorations can be created using open coils, as shown. To increase the variety, the length of paper can be folded at differing points and then open coils made in the ends.

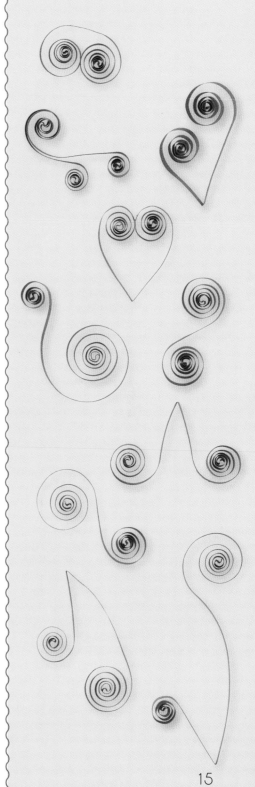

Further techniques

Like any craft, quilling has evolved over time and pioneering practitioners have pushed the boundaries forward to incorporate new tools and techniques. While these may not be considered to fall within the realms of 'pure' quilling, they do add variety and spice to quilled pieces. For more experienced quillers, it is always advantageous to have a range of techniques at your disposal when creating a new item or developing a design, since you can then select the most appropriate method to realize your ideas.

Fringing

I regard the fringing tool (see page 9) simply as a godsend. It allows you to fringe narrow strips of paper quickly and precisely, as opposed to fringing by hand, which is much more time-consuming and hard on the hands. Some fringing tools are adjustable so that you can fringe different widths of paper. The fringed strips can then be coiled or otherwise used to create flowers (see Dainty Daisy, page 45), hairy caterpillars (see page 35), feathers (see Feathered Hat, page 77), frondy leaves (see Carrot Bunch, page 24) and a frilly decoration for a wand (see page 61).

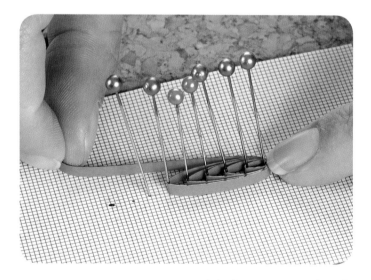

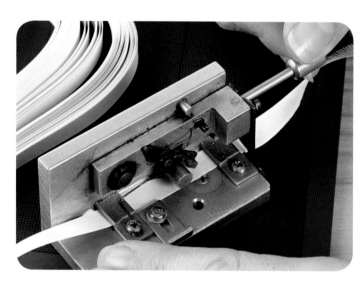

A 90 degree-angled fringing tool is being used here to fringe 10mm (⅜in) wide paper

Husking

This technique involves looping paper around pins inserted into a cork, foam, polystyrene or Styrofoam board, to create any shape you want in any size. Although it is simple to do, the results are wonderfully delicate, as in the Hovering Dragonfly, page 36. You can make a template showing the position of the pins, so that it can then be used to create identical items in whatever quantity you require.

In husking, paper strips are looped around carefully positioned pins inserted into a board

Spreuer

The Spreuer technique uses an onion holder (see page 10), which has a series of metal prongs around and through which paper is looped to create elaborate decorations, such as in Chic Shoe, page 78. The paper can be looped in numerous ways to produce a wide variety of designs.

This shows the use of the onion holder for the Spreuer technique to make a shoe bow

Weaving

Strips of paper of equal or differing widths can be woven together to make background papers or add textured elements to a quilled design, as in Delicious Ice Cream, page 87, where it is used to create the cone. Using precise, commercially cut quilling papers ensures that the woven effect is perfectly even. The colours used can also be selected to match the coils or shapes you are making with other techniques. Weaving shows how you can think laterally and use quilling papers in unexpected and creative ways.

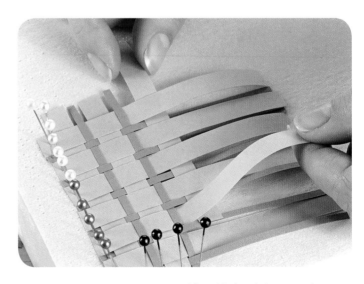

A foam block and pins are used to secure the strips of paper in place in the weaving technique

Protecting and preserving your quilling

Being made of paper and three-dimensional, quilled items are susceptible to damage over time. But taking a few simple precautionary measures will ensure that their condition is preserved. After all, if examples of quilled pieces have survived from Victorian times, then yours can surely last into the next century!

Fading

Paper will fade if it is placed in direct sunlight, and it is surprising how quickly it will do so. Here is an example of a quilled carrot that has faded from bright to pale orange after being placed on a windowsill. So keep your paper and quilled items away from sunlight to avoid such undesirable damaging effects.

Framing

A box frame that has a recess is ideal for displaying a quilled picture, as the coils are kept away from the glass. Otherwise, you can purchase a picture frame and discard the glass, but it will collect dust over time. Quilled pictures in box frames with or without glass will fade if they are placed where the direct sunlight will reach them, so position them with care.

Sprays

Some quillers use an acrylic spray sealant to protect their papers from fading and dust. These sprays have to be used carefully and it is always best to test them out on a spare piece of quilling first and leave it to dry to check that it doesn't have an adverse effect.

Recording designs

If you have worked hard on a quilled card or gift for somebody, you might find yourself feeling reluctant to give it to them! But one way of holding onto your best creations is to take a photograph of them for your records. Using a digital camera is an ideal method of compiling a catalogue of images of your quilled designs that you can store safely and compactly on disk, then easily access and view on a computer whenever you want.

You need to decide how precious your quilled work is and which are your favourite items that you want to record or try and preserve. I personally regard my quilling work as a continual process of evolution, and I don't always like to see my pieces from years ago. However, it can be interesting and valuable to chart your progress in quilling by preserving your work for the future.

Sending your quilled cards

Presentation of your quilled designs is important and extends to the way they are delivered. A special box or envelope provides the perfect finishing touch and ensures optimum condition. Make the box or envelope large enough to accommodate bubblewrap for extra protection.

Making a box

Tailor-making a box for your card will take only a few extra minutes and is sure to impress the recipient, especially if tied up with some pretty ribbon. Use strong card, around 300gsm in weight.

Fold and crease along the score lines.

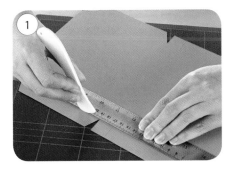

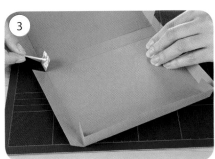

Enlarge the template on page 116 on a photocopier to the size you require. Cut along the outside solid lines, then draw around the template onto scrap card and cut out with a craft knife and metal ruler. Draw around the template onto your chosen card and cut out in the same way. Use the metal ruler and a scoring or embossing tool to score the lines indicated on the template.

Apply PVA (white) glue with a cocktail stick (toothpick) to each of the four tabs on the box base. Press these tabs to the inside of the box side to complete the box base. The lid will then fit neatly into the base.

Making an envelope

Alternatively, if you are hand-delivering the card, make an envelope to fit in a coordinating coloured strong paper or lightweight card. A quick way to do this is to use a plastic envelope maker, which allows you to make several sizes and shapes of envelope.

Follow the measurements given with the envelope maker and select the scoring lines needed on the plastic templates. Score a line along the groove by pressing the scoring tool through the paper into the groove. Turn the paper 180 degrees and score in the same groove, then turn 90 degrees and score in a different groove, as instructed, and finally turn 180 degrees to score a fourth line.

Remove the scored paper from the template and fold along the scored lines. Glue the bottom flap in place.

Projects

Cooking capers, page 96

Baby talk, page 54

Fab fashion, page 74

Animal magic, page 62

Beautiful bugs, page 30

Beach life, page 82

Nicely nautical, page 90

Gardening gems, page 22

Flower power, page 38

Christmas crackers, page 106

Fairy fantasy, page 58

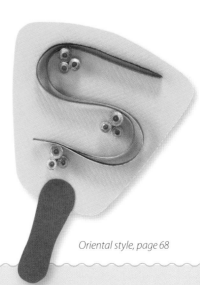

Wonderful weddings, page 48

Party time, page 102

Oriental style, page 68

Gardening gems

Cultivate the perennial interests of your green-fingered friends and family yet further with some prize-winning papercrafted produce. These delightful quilled items can be used to transform everyday utilitarian items, such as a seed box or a plant pot or vase, into unique gifts with equal appeal to both sexes.

Handy secateurs page 29

Timeless topiary page 28

Tasty tomatoes page 25

Sweet peas page 25

Carrot bunch page 24

Artful onion page 27

Trusty trowel and fork page 26

Carrot bunch

Each of these crunchy-looking carrots, complete with lush green leafy tops, is formed from a paper strip coiled into a cone. All are made with 20cm (8in) lengths of paper, which demonstrates how the way in which you coil can alter the size and shape of the resulting cone. For extra touches of realism, the cones are made slightly unevenly and soil is used to colour them.

You will need

- 3mm (⅛in) wide orange paper
- 10mm (⅜in) wide green paper
- soil
- 45 degree-angled fringing tool
- snips (optional)
- Basic Tool Kit (see page 8)

For the carrot roots, cut a 1.3cm (½in) length of the orange paper into four very narrow strands, but leave them joined at the end. Glue to the end of a 20cm (8in) length of orange paper for the carrot itself.

Position the quilling tool to the left of the strands, with the strands hanging downwards, and begin to turn the tool to coil the paper tightly for a few turns.

TIP

Customs regulations prohibit the transport of soil internationally so if you are sending your quilled carrots abroad, use felt-tip pen to colour them instead.

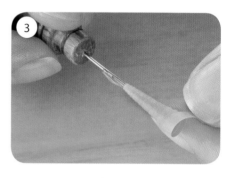

Continue turning the quilling tool, but as you do so, angle the paper away from the tool so that as you coil it creates a cone shape. When coiling, make sure that the paper overlaps, but vary the overlaps to make the cone uneven. Secure the end of the paper with glue. Apply a generous coating of glue inside the cone with a cocktail stick (toothpick) and leave to dry.

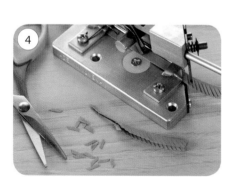

For the leaves, fold a length of the green paper in half along its length and use the fringing tool to fringe. Cut the fringed paper into 5cm (2in) lengths. Keeping the paper folded in half, trim the fringes for a length of 1.5cm (⅝in) from one end, leaving the uncut margin as a stalk.

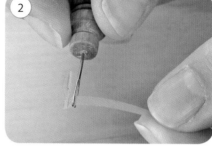

Using small scissors or snips, make random cuts into the fringing before unfolding and opening the paper strip. Round the tip of the leaf. You will need three or four leaves per carrot.

Glue the leaf stalks to the end of a 10cm (4in) length of orange paper and start coiling from the end with the leaves. Make a tight coil. Apply a generous amount of glue inside the top of the carrot cone, then insert the tight coil. Add real soil to the carrots and trim the ends of the roots to make them look as realistic as possible.

Sweet peas and tasty tomatoes

These luscious vegetables are quick and easy to make, and it is highly satisfying to see a pile of them growing on your work surface. Both are created using tight coils, the tomatoes using a longer length of the paper for a larger result. The coils are pushed up slightly to achieve a domed effect.

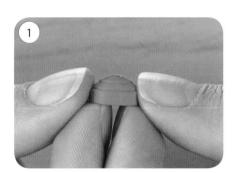

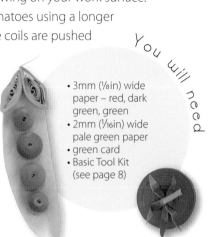

You will need

- 3mm (⅛in) wide paper – red, dark green, green
- 2mm (¹⁄₁₆in) wide pale green paper
- green card
- Basic Tool Kit (see page 8)

To make a tomato, glue two 40cm (15¾in) lengths of red paper together end to end. Make a tight coil and glue the end in place. Push the inner edge of the coil out with your fingernail. Be careful not to push the centre of the coil out, as this makes the shape too high.

Apply a generous amount of glue inside the tomato, taking great care not to change the shape. Leave to dry.

Cut tiny leaves from the dark green paper. To make stalks, glue two lengths of the dark green paper together lengthways and leave to dry. Cut in half lengthways and trim to 1cm (⅜in) lengths. Glue a stalk and three or four leaves to the top of each tomato – they will crumple to realistic effect in the process.

For the peas, make tight closed coils with 20cm (8in) and 30cm (12in) lengths of the green paper, then push out the inner edge of each coil and glue inside, as in Step 1. For the leaves, make loose closed coils from 20cm (8in) lengths of the pale green paper, then pinch into eye shapes (see page 14). Glue a short strand of the paper in the centre. Using the template on page 116, cut a pea pod from green card, then score and gently fold down the centre. Glue the peas to the centre of the pod and the leaves at one end.

TIP
If you find it difficult to use your fingernail to push out the inner edges of the coils, use the rounded end of a pen or a similar object.

INSPIRATIONS

Carrot cupcake
Celebrate a veggie-lover's birthday with this novel card design, featuring a carrot cake with a difference, decorated with a pile of simple open coils and topped with a colourful carrot. See page 116 for the cupcake template.

Pod pairing
Here, two pea pods adorn a wooden plant label, which would make a lovely gift for a vegetable grower combined with a seed tray and a selection of suitable seed packets. Alternatively, they could be used to decorate the cover of a gardening journal, diary or calendar.

Tomato trio
Three quilled tomatoes mounted onto squares of contrasting pale-coloured card are positioned in a row for a stylish, contemporary-style tag to make a gardening gift extra special. Note that the central tomato's stalk and leaves are glued to the edge of the coil for added interest.

25

Trusty trowel and fork

These matching mini gardening tools are irresistibly intriguing, with their realistic 3-D handles formed from brown paper strips coiled into cone shapes, to which simple card shapes for the trowel or fork blades are attached. All you need is a little practice to sharpen up your hand-eye coordination and apply the correct degree of tension to create short, stubby cone shapes.

You will need

- 3mm (⅛in) wide paper in two shades of brown
- card – silver, black
- Basic Tool Kit (see page 8)

1

Insert one end of a 20cm (8in) length of one of the brown papers into your quilling tool. Coil tightly for three turns.

2

Continue turning the quilling tool, but as you do so, angle the paper away from the tool so that as you coil it creates a cone shape. You need to make sure that the paper overlaps as you coil.

3

Continue coiling away from the tool until you reach near to the end of the paper. For the final 2cm (¾in), coil without angling the paper away from the tool to create a flat top. Carefully remove the quilling tool and secure the end of the paper with glue. Use a cocktail stick (toothpick) to apply a generous coating of glue inside the cone shape, right down to the bottom, to give it some rigidity when dry.

4

Using a medium-sized pair of scissors, cut a 15cm (6in) length of the same brown paper in half along its length, thereby creating two 1.5mm (1/16in) wide pieces.

5

Use one of the 1.5mm (1/16in) wide pieces of brown paper to make a tight closed coil, which will form a 'plug' for the end of the cone. Apply a generous amount of glue inside the top of the cone and insert the tight closed coil.

TIP

The exact size of the cones will vary depending on how much you overlap the paper as you coil, so it's a good idea to make a batch of cones and closed coil 'plugs', then see which fit together the best.

6

Using the template on page 116, cut a trowel blade from silver card. Using a scoring tool against a metal ruler, score a line down the centre. Fold along the score line, then open out to leave a slight fold. Glue to the handle. Make the fork in same way, using the other brown paper for the handle and cutting the fork blade from black card (template on page 116).

Artful onion

Different quilling techniques are combined here to great effect. The main part of the onion uses lengths of paper joined together to make a large coil with the quilling tool, which is only slightly released and then pinched into shape, while the leaves are formed into loops by hand.

You will need

- 3mm (⅛in) wide paper – pale brown, green, dark brown
- Basic Tool Kit (see page 8)

Glue four 40cm (15¾in) lengths of the pale brown paper together end to end. Make a tight coil, but release it a fraction before gluing the end in place. Keep holding the coil.

TIP
The onion may look as though it has two shades of brown, but this is because each side of the paper is a very slightly different colour due to the way it has been cut. This only adds to the realistic effect.

Continue holding the coil while spreading glue onto one side; if you release the coil before gluing, the centre will spring outwards and it will lose its evenness. Pinch the top of the coil when the glue has dried.

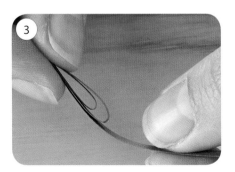

Form a 20cm (8in) length of the green paper into a loop 1.5cm (⅝in) high. Then make another loop around the first loop and repeat twice more.

While still holding the loops, cut through the bottom of the loops. Place glue on all the ends and attach to the top of the onion. Cut tiny leaves from the dark brown paper and glue to the bottom of the onion to resemble roots.

INSPIRATIONS

Key tools
This clear plastic key ring has a 2mm (¹⁄₁₆in) wide recess, in which the trowel and fork set has been placed. The cones for the handles are squashed slightly, but this serves to hold them in place and prevent them from moving around inside the key ring.

Notable bulb
Make a gift something to remember – literally – by creating this smart holder for mini stick-on notes for all those cultivation or cooking reminders. The quilled onion is simply mounted onto layered cream, checked and orange card – a scheme that will fit in well with any kitchen or garden shed setting. The same design could be used for a thank you or birthday card.

Timeless topiary

Topiary has many attractive stylized shapes and forms that can be successfully imitated in quilling to produce some wonderfully textural, sophisticated designs with wide appeal. Although the bushes need a lot of pinched coils, they are easy to make and won't take long to create once you get into the coiling rhythm.

You will need

• 3mm (⅛in) wide paper – green, red
• brown card
• white inkpad
• cotton bud
• adhesive foam pads
• Basic Tool Kit (see page 8)

Snip lengths of the green paper between 3cm (1⅛in) and 7cm (2¾in) in order to create a variety of different-sized leaves.

TIP

These topiary pots are ideal for decorating doll's houses.

Use the lengths of green paper to make loose closed coils and then pinch at two opposing points to create leaf shapes. Place in a container or a shallow lid to prevent them from getting lost on your work desk.

Using the templates on page 117, cut plant pots from brown card. Press a cotton bud into the white inkpad, then lightly run it down the edges of the plant pots. Repeat several times to achieve the desired effect of aged terracotta.

Place an adhesive foam pad on the back of each plant pot, remove the backing paper and then place another adhesive foam pad on top, to create a double thickness. Position on the card or other surface you are decorating.

Make tight closed coils with 2–3cm (¾–1⅛in) lengths of the red paper. Pick up a coil with tweezers and add glue to one side or dip into glue, then position on the card or other surface above the pot. Use about seven coils for the small pot and 13 for the larger pot, but you can make some bushes without the red coils.

Glue the leaves around the red coils, working upwards and filling the bush shape as you go. Some leaves can be placed on their side in order to vary the effect slightly.

Handy secateurs

The handles of this cute cutting tool are made using the same technique as for the carrots and the trowel and fork (see pages 24 and 26), but here the overlap is smaller to create a narrow cone shape. The cone is quite fragile and so requires a very delicate touch when handling until the glue applied to the inside is dry.

You will need

- 3mm (⅛in) wide paper – cream, brown
- black card
- Basic Tool Kit (see page 8)

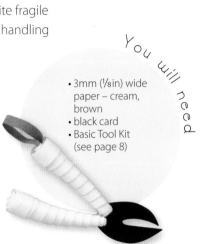

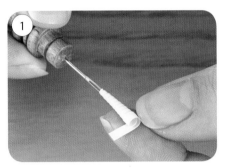

Insert a 9cm (3½in) length of the cream paper into your quilling tool. Turn the tool, and as you do so, angle the paper away from the tool, as in Step 1, page 26, but with very small overlaps. Glue the end in place and then place glue inside the cone, as in Step 3, page 26. Repeat to make a second cone.

2

When the glue has dried, bend the cones slightly with your fingers.

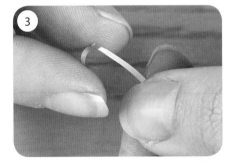

3

Cut a 4.5cm (1¾in) length of cream paper in half lengthways and glue a 1cm (⅜in) piece of brown paper in a loop to one end. Start coiling from the end with the loop and make a tight closed coil.

4

Insert the coil into the end of one cone shape. Make another tight closed coil but without the loop and insert this into the other cone. Using the template on page 117, cut two secateurs blades from black card. Apply glue to the blades and then the ends of the cones and stick in position.

TIP

These cones are a little challenging to make, but once mastered, you can use the technique to make shears (see Shear Delight right), a skipping rope, decorator's paintbrush or a saucepan.

INSPIRATIONS

Pots of style

Two smaller topiary bushes flank a larger one to make an attractive arrangement for this versatile card design. You could dress it up by using metallic-edged papers for the coils (see page 6) and adding gem stones for Christmas.

Pruning pleasure

The secateurs are mounted onto a lime green gift tag tied with raffia for a rustic finishing touch. Team with the topiary to inspire some creative cutting!

Shear delight

Here, an aperture was cut in a small green card and correspondingly in green striped paper, then glued together with a sheet of acetate in between. The shears, made in the same way as the secateurs (template on page 117), are glued onto the acetate and raffia tied around the card spine.

Beautiful bugs

The insect world offers a fascinating variety of colourful, delicate and intricate forms on a miniature scale – qualities also inherent in quilling, making it the ideal medium for re-creating these characterful creatures. Adults and children alike are guaranteed to be intrigued and amused by these quilled curiosities.

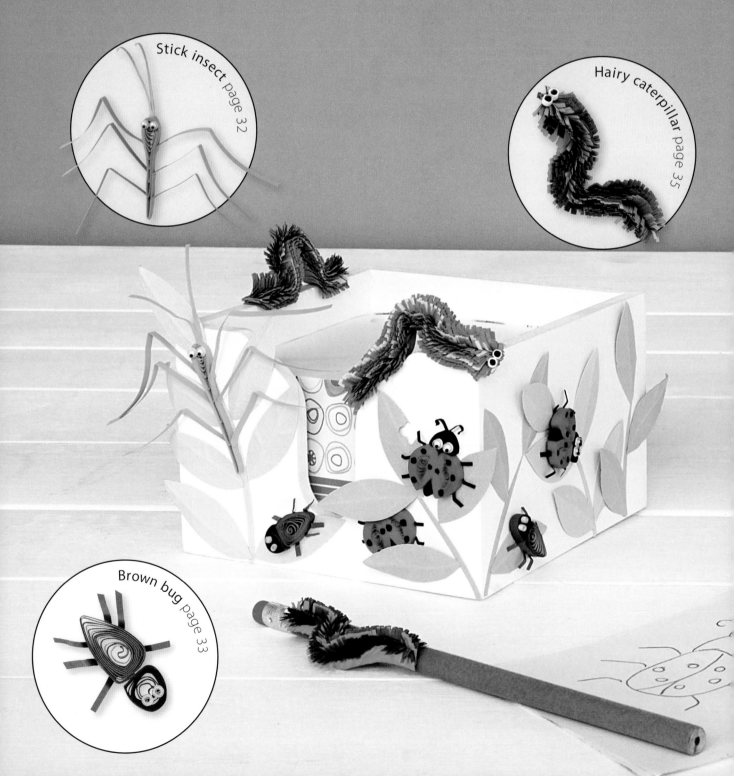

Stick insect page 32

Hairy caterpillar page 35

Brown bug page 33

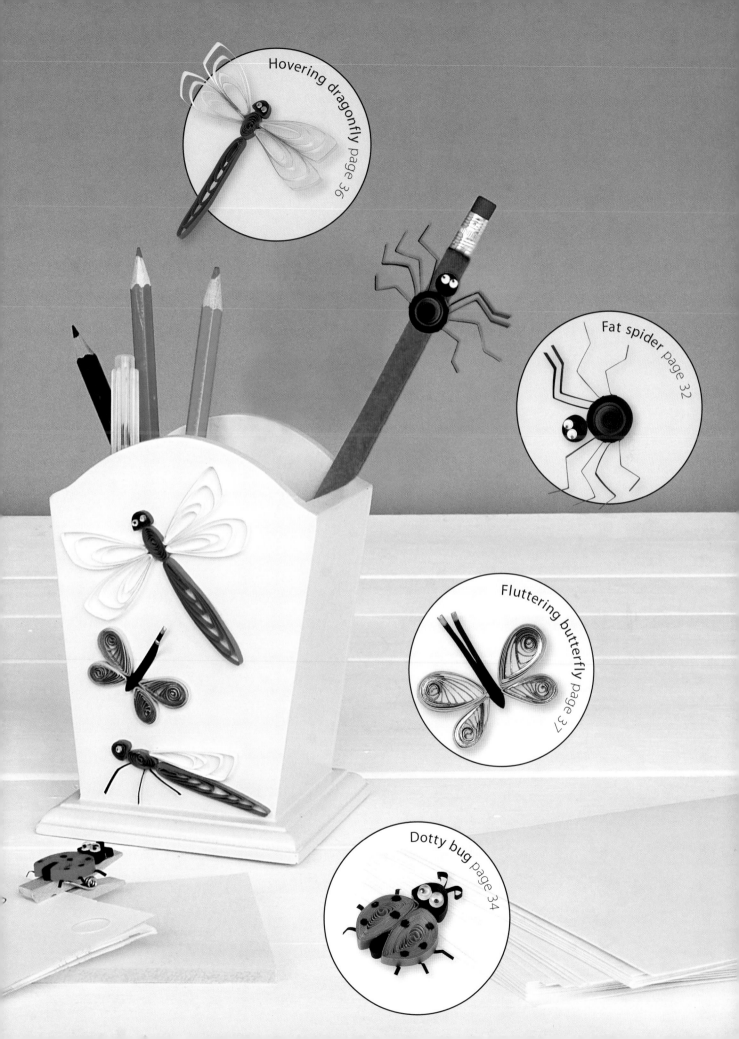

Hovering dragonfly page 36

Fat spider page 32

Fluttering butterfly page 37

Dotty bug page 34

Fat spider and stick insect

These insects may be contrasting in their proportions, but their bodies are made in the same way, from loose closed coils – very loose in the case of the stick insect and then squeezed and glued to hold. Both have long, thin legs, and these are easily created by making appropriate folds in paper strips and curling with your fingernail into just the right shape.

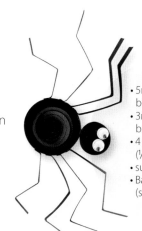

You will need

- 5mm (³⁄₁₆ in) wide black paper
- 3mm (⅛ in) wide bright green paper
- 4 wiggly eyes, 2mm (¹⁄₁₆ in) in diameter
- superglue
- Basic Tool Kit (see page 8)

To make the spider, for the body, glue two 40cm (15¾ in) lengths of the black paper end to end and make a loose closed coil. For the head, make a smaller loose closed coil with a 40cm (15¾ in) length of the same paper and then glue to the body.

For the legs, cut six 4cm (1½ in) and two 3cm (1⅛ in) lengths of the black paper. Make a fold 3mm (⅛ in) from one end and then two more folds in each length, alternating the direction of the folds.

Place a small dot of glue on the 3mm (⅛ in) folded piece and glue to the body. Glue four legs on each side, with the slightly smaller ones at the back.

Pick up a wiggly eye with tweezers and apply superglue to the underside, then position on one side of the head. Add the other eye in the same way.

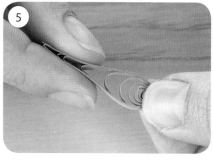

For the stick insect, make a very loose closed coil with a 40cm (15¾ in) length of the bright green paper. With your fingertips, pull the centre of the coil to one side and pinch the opposing side. When you let go, this will make a teardrop shape, so when you glue it to your chosen surface, you will need to squeeze it into a thin shape, apply glue all the way along and hold in place for a few seconds while the glue dries.

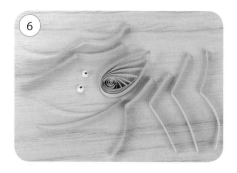

For the legs, cut four 6cm (2½ in) and two 5cm (2in) lengths of the green paper. Make a fold 2mm (¹⁄₁₆ in) from one end and another fold halfway along. Glue to the body using the 2mm (¹⁄₁₆ in) fold. For antennae, cut a 4.5cm (1¾ in) length of the paper in half lengthways and glue to the body. Attach two wiggly eyes, as in Step 4.

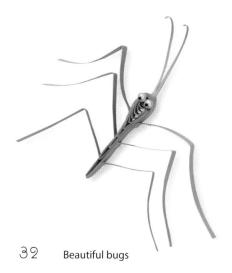

Brown bug

Even bugs become cute when quilled! The body of this tiny brown beast is created by coiling two shades of paper together at once to produce a loose coil with an interesting two-tone effect. The same technique can be applied to flowers.

You will need

- 3mm (⅛in) wide paper – pale brown, dark brown, mid brown, pale cream
- Basic Tool Kit (see page 8)

For the body, glue a 20cm (8in) length of the pale brown paper to a 20cm (8in) length of the dark brown at one end.

Start coiling both pieces together, making sure that the dark brown paper is on the outside. Continue coiling until the other ends are reached. The paler brown paper will now be longer than the dark brown, so trim the excess and then make a loose closed coil by gluing the ends in place.

Pinch the body coil at one end and flatten the other end to make a flat teardrop shape. For the head, make a loose closed coil with a 15cm (6in) length of the mid brown paper and then pinch into an elongated crescent shape (see page 14). Glue to the body.

For the eyes, make tight closed coils with two 2cm (¾in) lengths of the pale cream paper. Use tweezers to dip into glue, then position on the head. For the legs, cut two 1.5cm (⅝in) lengths of mid brown paper, then cut each lengthways into three very thin strands and follow Steps 5–6 of Dotty Bug, page 34, to attach and trim.

TIP
These bugs don't have to be brown – they could be green, black or dark red.

INSPIRATIONS

Web wonder
This vibrant orange-coloured notebook is decorated with a silver glitter glue spider's web. Two quilled brown bugs are caught up in the web, while the big fat spider sits watchfully in the corner!

Insect jar
Encourage children in their curiosity about the wonderful world of insects with this jam jar containing a stick insect that looks as though it's equally curious in return, topped by a piece of red gingham fabric secured with a rubber band. For an extra realistic touch, cut some leaves from pale green card (template on page 117), score and fold down the centre, then attach either side of a green card stem.

Bugged tag
Give someone an enjoyably scary surprise with this insect-infested tag. A trio of quilled bugs are simply mounted onto a wooden tag with a decorative faux stitched edging and tied with paper string.

Dotty bug

A quickly assembled combination of pinched loose coils creates this charming little ladybird (ladybug) to cheer up any card, tag or stationery item. The insect's characteristic dots are speedily added too, just by drawing them on with felt-tip pen.

You will need

- 3mm (⅛in) wide paper – red, black
- 2 wiggly eyes, 2mm (¹⁄₁₆in) in diameter
- superglue
- black felt-tip pen
- Basic Tool Kit (see page 8)

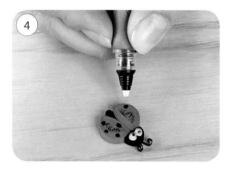

For the body, make two slightly loose tight coils with 60cm (23¾in) lengths of the red paper. Pinch into crescent shapes (see page 14). Make a loose closed coil with a 5cm (2in) length of the black paper and pinch into a teardrop shape (see page 14). Glue all three shapes together as shown, holding in place while the glue dries.

For the head, make a loose closed coil with a 20cm (8in) length of the black paper and pinch into a crescent shape. Glue to the body and attach two small wiggly eyes with superglue.

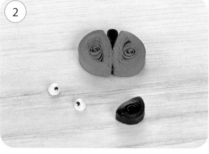

For the antennae, cut a 1.5cm (¹⁄₁₆in) length of the black paper in half lengthways. Fold one piece in half, then coil both ends outwards to the fold. Glue to the head.

Draw spots on the red paper with the black pen. The ink is likely to spread or 'bleed', so either test on a spare shape or proceed slowly. Add as many spots as you wish, but make sure that the wings are symmetrical.

TIP
You don't have to add the legs, as it could be a resting ladybird.

For the legs, cut three 1cm (⅜in) lengths of the black paper, then cut each length lengthways into three. Glue to the underside of the ladybird, three legs on each side.

Turn the ladybird over and fold the legs upwards. Trim the ends of the legs so that they are in proportion and at an angle.

Hairy caterpillar

The fringing technique is usually associated with making frilly flowers, but here it is inventively applied to create a realistic hairy effect for this creeping caterpillar, using multiple fringed lengths in two different colours glued together and then spread out.

- 10mm (³⁄₈in) wide paper – green and yellow or brown and orange
- 2mm (¹⁄₁₆in) wide paper – black, white
- 90 degree-angled fringing tool
- Basic Tool Kit (see page 8)

Well pegged
The lovable quilled ladybird has been attached to a mini wooden peg to make an endearing gift for a nature lover. It would be useful for sealing half-used seed packets, so present it with a couple, or clip it onto a notepad.

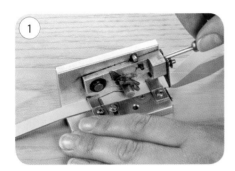

Fringe two 45cm (18in) lengths of the 10mm (³⁄₈in) wide papers in two different colours, green and yellow or brown and orange. In some fringing tools, you can fringe two pieces at once to save time.

Cut the fringed pieces into 7cm (2³⁄₄in) lengths. Glue these together at the uncut margin, alternating the colours as follows: five of green or brown, one of yellow or orange, five of green or brown, one of yellow or orange, five of green or brown. Make sure that they are glued all the way along the margin.

TIP
All pieces of the caterpillar must be glued thoroughly, otherwise when you bend it, gaps will show in the unglued sections.

Creepy crawly pencil
Make a child squirm with delight with this caterpillar-enhanced pencil. Alternatively, he could be seen creeping over a pencil box or the cover of a notebook. This tactile insect would also, being quilled rather than real, make a welcome gift for a grown-up gardener.

Push the fringe out all the way along to make the caterpillar fluffy. Trim a few pieces from one end to make space for the eyes.

For the eyes, glue a 2cm (³⁄₄in) length of the black paper to 3cm (1¹⁄₈in) of the white. Start coiling from the black end and make a tight closed coil. Repeat for the other eye. Glue to the trimmed head.

Hovering dragonfly

The intricate, airy quality of this glamorous insect's wings and the fineness of its body are achieved by using the husking technique (see page 16), whereby the quilling paper is wrapped around pins inserted into a board.

You will need

- 3mm (⅛in) wide paper – white, blue edged with metallic blue
- tiny yellow gem stones or beads
- cork or foam board and pins
- masking tape (optional)
- Basic Tool Kit (see page 8)

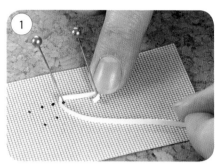

For the wing, photocopy or trace the template on page 117. Place on a cork or foam board. Hold in position with masking tape or pins at the corners. Insert a pin at points 1 and 2. Fold over 3mm (⅛in) at one end of a length of the white paper. Loop around pin 1 and take the other end to pin 2 and wrap around. Add a dot of glue at this end and secure the paper to it.

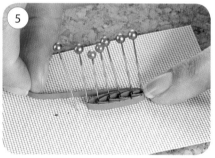

Insert a pin at point 3. Take the end of the paper around this pin and back to pin 1. Add a dot of glue at the base. Insert a pin at points 4 and 5.

Take the paper around pins 4 and 5, then glue at the base. Insert a pin at points 6 and 7, wrap the paper around and glue at the base. Trim the excess paper. Make three more wings in this way, plus one for the resting dragonfly, if required (see Winged Delight opposite).

For the body, photocopy or trace the template on page 117 and place on the cork or foam board, as in Step 1. Insert a pin at points 1 and 2. Fold over 3mm (⅛in) at one end of a length of the metallic-edged blue paper. Loop around pin 1, take the other end to pin 2 and wrap around, then glue at the base. Insert a pin at point 3 and wrap around.

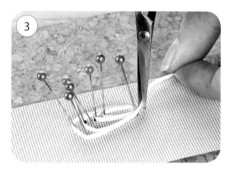

Insert the remaining pins, following the template for positioning, and wrap the paper around, as for the wings.

For the head, make a loose closed coil with a 10cm (4in) length of the metallic-edged blue paper and pinch into a crescent shape (see page 14). For the upper body, make a loose closed coil from a 15cm (6in) length of the blue paper and gently pinch in the centre. Glue the head and body parts to your chosen surface, then glue on the wings either side. Add gem stones for eyes or use beads.

Fluttering butterfly

Everyone's favourite insect, both the body and wing parts of this beautiful butterfly are simply formed from loose closed coils pinched into shape, the latter using metallic-edged paper for a shimmering effect. Silver 3-D paint adds dimension and sheen to the antennae.

You will need

- 3mm (1/8in) wide paper – black, purple edged with metallic purple, purple
- silver 3-D paint
- Basic Tool Kit (see page 8)

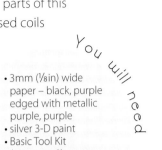

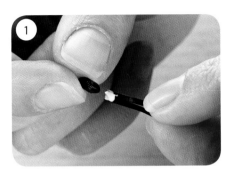

1 For the body, make a loose closed coil with an 8cm (3in) length of the black paper and pinch at two opposing points. Cut a 2cm (3/4in) length of the black paper in half lengthways for 1.5cm (5/8in). Glue the uncut part to the body.

3 For the wings, make two loose closed coils from 15cm (6in) lengths of the metallic-edged purple paper glued to 20cm (8in) lengths of plain purple and another two with 15cm (6in) lengths of metallic-edged purple paper glued to 10cm (4in) lengths of plain purple. Pinch each into a teardrop shape (see page 14) and glue to either side of the body, with the smaller shapes at the bottom.

2 Glue the body and antennae to your chosen surface.

4 Add dots of silver 3-D paint to the ends of the antennae and leave to dry; squirt some of the paint out onto scrap paper first to get it flowing and to gauge how hard to press the tube.

TIP
While 3-D paint adds desirable dimension here, it takes a relatively long time to dry, so use silver pen if you have to fly!

Winged delight
A gossamer-winged blue dragonfly appears to hover over a green specimen resting below – for this variation, just make one wing, and attach three legs, as for the ladybird (see page 35, Steps 5–6). This card is sure to enchant any nature lover or budding entomologist.

Captured beauty
Here, the hovering butterfly is framed by a circle of green card, mounted onto a larger purple circle trimmed with matching ribbon to make a dainty tag for a prettily packaged gift. You could also combine the butterfly motif with the quilled garden flowers on page 40 to make a lovely summery card design.

Flower power

Flowers and foliage have a universal appeal and make suitable subjects for so many occasions. What's more, flowers and quilling go hand in hand, since the delicate quality of quilled paper naturally forms floral shapes. The colours and varieties of real flowers can offer endless inspiration for quilled designs.

Dazzling daffodil page 43

Dainty daisy page 45

Bobbing bluebell page 42

Looped leaves page 46

Fabulous flower head page 41

Frilly flower page 44

Garden flowers page 40

Pretty petals page 47

Garden flowers

These flowers are an ideal introduction to the coiling and pinching techniques of quilling, but they also involve an extra refinement, where the inner parts of the coil are manipulated before being pinched. In this way, you can ensure that each petal is prettily formed.

You will need

• 3mm (⅛in) wide paper – orange, pink or red, green
• quilling board (optional)
• Basic Tool Kit (see page 8)

Make loose closed coils with 40cm (15¾in) lengths of the orange paper. Here, a quilling board (see page 10) has been used to ensure that the coils are the same size, using the 2cm (¾in) diameter template.

Before pinching the coils into regular teardrop shapes to create petals (see page 14), pull the centre of each coil to one side and flex the coil to make the spaces between the inner parts even, then pinch so that the join is at the pointed end.

Glue a 10cm (4in) length of the pink or red paper to an equal length of the green paper end to end. Make a tight coil, starting at the pink or red and stopping at the green. Glue in position on the card or other surface you are decorating to form a flower centre and an adjoining stem.

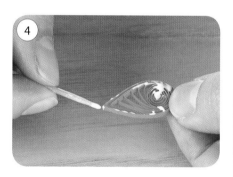

Apply glue all over the underside of one petal and at the point, but take care not to smother it with glue.

Adhere the petal to one side of the flower centre, with the pointed end butting up to the coil. Glue another petal opposite the first one, if making a six-petalled flower. Then glue on another two petals at a time opposite each other.

The smaller flower is made with five 20cm (8in) lengths of orange paper for petals but with the same size flower centre as in Step 3. The coils are then pinched with the join at the rounded end and glued pointed-end outwards around the flower centre. Pinch two loose closed coils made with 20cm (8in) lengths of green paper for each flower into leaf shapes and glue either side of the stems.

TIP

If you don't have a quilling board, draw a circle on a piece of card and use as a guide to size.

Fabulous flower head

Although quilling is in its nature three-dimensional, there is no reason not to create additional depth by making two layers of coiled shapes. For this showy-looking flower head, an upper layer of smaller petal shapes has been glued on top of the base layer of larger petals, allowing the light to pass through.

You will need

• 2mm (1/16in) wide paper in two shades of deep pink
• 5mm (3/16in) wide yellow paper
• quilling board
• Basic Tool Kit (see page 8)

Make loose closed coils from eight 40cm (15¾in) lengths of one shade of pink paper. Pinch each coil to make eye shapes (see page 14). Use the 2cm (¾in) diameter template of a quilling board to ensure that all the coils are the same size.

Make a loose closed coil from a 5cm (2in) length of the yellow paper for the flower centre. Make a mark with a pencil on your chosen surface where you want to position the flower centre and glue the coil over this.

TIP

You can use 3mm (1/8in) wide papers for both layers for an alternative, chunkier result.

Make smaller loose closed coils from 20cm (8in) lengths of the other shade of pink paper, using the 1.3cm (½in) diameter template of the quilling board to ensure that they are all the same size. Pinch as in Step 1. Glue to the top of the first set of petals to create a second layer.

Arrange the petals around the flower centre first, to make sure that they fit and are positioned evenly, then glue in place.

Sun flowers

These simple yet striking orange quilled flowers, glued onto pale orange card and then mounted onto a deeper orange single-fold card, are guaranteed to bring warmth and cheer to their recipient. The smaller flower could be used to create a coordinating gift tag.

In full bloom

This luxurious double-layered bloom, glued to a circle of pale pink card, makes a great tag for a Mother's Day gift. The satin ribbon loop is attached by backing the tag with a second circle of card and sandwiching it in between. The design could be adapted to make an intriguing brooch or colourful fridge magnet, or used to decorate a gift box.

Bobbing bluebell

The technique of coiling paper into a cone shape used for the carrots and trowel and fork set on pages 24 and 26 is adapted here to form a bell shape and to realistically re-create this delightfully delicate wild flower in paper. The end of a 10mm (⅜in) wide strip is snipped into points and then the remainder trimmed lengthways before coiling to create the decorative lip of the bluebell.

You will need

- 10mm (⅜in) wide mauve paper
- scrap of yellow paper
- green paper
- Basic Tool Kit (see page 8)

Cut eight points in one end of a 30cm (12in) length of the mauve paper.

TIP
You can vary the size of the overlaps to create bluebells of slightly differing sizes for a naturalistic look.

Trim the remaining length of the paper strip to leave it 3mm (⅛in) wide.

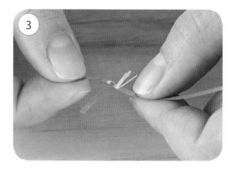

Glue about four narrow strands of yellow paper to the other end of the mauve strip from the points but on the same side as the points. Cut a stem and leaf from the mauve paper, then glue opposite the yellow strands.

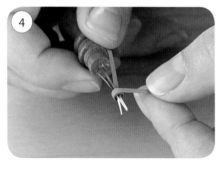

Starting from the yellow strands end, make a tight coil, allowing the stem and leaf to hang downwards, keeping the coil flat to begin with but for more turns than for the carrots (see step 2, page 24) to create a wider base.

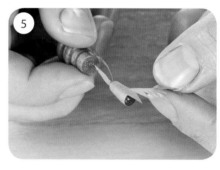

Continue coiling to the points, but angle the paper away from the tool, making sure that the paper overlaps. Glue the end of the paper in place.

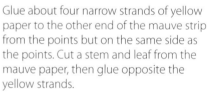

Using the quilling tool, coil each of the eight points outwards without gluing. Apply glue to the inside of the bell shape with a cocktail stick (toothpick), then leave to dry. Glue the flower stem to a 3mm (⅛in) wide length of green paper and allow the flower leaf to hang free. Cut a tapered leaf from green paper. Trim the green stem to the length you require and attach the leaf before gluing in place on the card or other surface.

Dazzling daffodil

The trumpet of this gloriously bold flower, which traditionally heralds the coming of spring, is again formed by using the coiled cone technique but in a chunkier guise. The wider base provides the foundation for building the cone upwards and outwards, with the decorative edge, snipped with fancy-edged scissors, supplying the finishing touch.

You will need

- 10mm (⅜in) wide paper – yellow, orange, green
- 3mm (⅛in) wide yellow paper
- green paper
- fancy-edged scissors
- Basic Tool Kit (see page 8)

1 Cut along the edge of a strip of the 10mm (⅜in) wide yellow paper using fancy-edged scissors.

2 Glue a 20cm (8in) length of the same yellow paper to a 40cm (15¾in) length end to end, then glue a 10cm (4in) length of the fancy-edged strip to the end of this. For stamens, cut four strips of the orange paper about 1mm x 1.5cm (¹⁄₁₆ x ⅝in) and glue to the plain end.

3 Starting at the plain end, make a tight coil for a length of about 20cm (8in), then angle the paper away from the tool, making sure that it overlaps, to form a cone shape. This becomes quite a challenge towards the end, so coil slowly and carefully. Glue the end in place.

TIP
Make a narcissus instead by gluing white petals around a yellow trumpet.

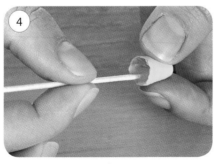

4 Move the orange stamens to one side and use a cocktail stick (toothpick) to apply glue inside the trumpet around the side. Leave to dry. For the petals, make five loose closed coils from 30cm (12in) lengths of the 3mm (⅛in) wide yellow paper pinched into teardrop shapes (see page 14), then pull the points of the inner parts in line with the pinched point when glued to the card or other surface. For the stem, glue two lengths of the 10mm (⅜in) wide green paper together lengthways, and then cut a long narrow leaf with one pointed end from green paper.

INSPIRATIONS

Planter's plaque
A spray of four bluebells is mounted onto a square of cream card layered onto a slightly larger square of mauve card and in turn attached to the top of a blue wooden plant label to make a lovely gift for a flower lover – especially in conjunction with a potted indoor plant or a pretty plant plot and bulbs for planting. You could add an appropriate message to the cream card.

Springtime special
In this elegant design, a single quilled daffodil makes a strong impact in its very simplicity, set against a pale green background and mounted onto a paler green, slightly textured single-fold card. Besides being ideal for celebrating Easter, it would bring an ailing friend or relative great comfort as a get well card.

Frilly flower

Create a big impact with this flamboyant flower, which is deceptively quick and easy to make using fringed paper. And the moment when you push the fringe out to reveal the flower is guaranteed to deliver just as much wow factor to you as to the recipient. In this case, the fringing is cut by hand, but pre-fringed papers are available for an even speedier result.

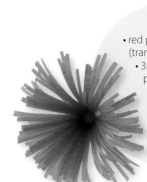

- red parchment (translucent) paper
- 3mm (⅛in) wide pink paper
- bulldog clip, 6cm (2⅜in) wide
- Basic Tool Kit (see page 8)

1

Cut a strip of the red paper 3 x 20cm (1⅛ x 8in). Fold the length into three and secure with the bulldog clip along one long edge.

2

Using a pair of scissors, make cuts all along the paper 1.5mm (¹⁄₁₆in) apart, finishing 3mm (⅛in) from the secured edge to leave a narrow uncut margin.

3

Remove the bulldog clip and unfold the fringed strip. Using scissors, make cuts where the folds were as in Step 2 so that the entire strip is evenly fringed.

TIP

The width of the paper used for fringing can be varied to achieve larger (up to 15cm/6in in diameter) or smaller flowers, as desired, and any papers – not just purpose-designed quilling papers – can be used.

4

Cut a 15cm (6in) length of the pink paper. Glue to the uncut margin at one end of the red fringed strip. Insert the end of the pink paper into your quilling tool and coil tightly until you reach the end of the red fringed strip, to form the flower centre. Glue the end in place.

5

Use your fingers to spread the fringe out to form the flower, then use your little finger to push the pink centre up slightly.

6

Gently drag your fingernail along the underside of each fringed 'petal' so that the paper curls under slightly.

Dainty daisy

These delightfully delicate daisies are made using a specially designed fringing tool (see page 9). This wonderful invention allows you to fringe lengths of paper quickly and easily, thus avoiding hand- and eye-strain, and produces perfect, evenly spaced cuts, ensuring that each flower is identical every time.

You will need

- 10mm (³⁄₈in) wide white paper
- 3mm (¹⁄₈in) wide papers – yellow, dark green
- 90 degree-angled fringing tool
- pink felt-tip pen
- Basic Tool Kit (see page 8)

1 Insert a 45cm (17³⁄₄in) length of the white paper into the fringing tool. Fringe the paper by moving the handle up and down. Continue until the whole length of the paper is fringed.

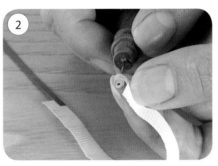

2 Remove the paper from the tool and check that there are no uncut areas. Cut a piece 12cm (4³⁄₄in) long. Glue a 12cm (4³⁄₄in) length of the yellow paper to the uncut margin at one end of the fringed strip and a 5cm (2in) length of the green paper to the other end in the same way. Insert the yellow paper into your quilling tool and coil tightly until you reach the green paper. Glue in place.

3 Use your fingers to spread out the fringe to form a flower shape. Gently brush the fringed ends of the flower with a pink felt-tip pen. Do this before the flowers are glued to your chosen surface, and make sure that you wash any pen off your hands.

TIP
To make the stems of the daisies stronger, glue two lengths of dark green 3mm (¹⁄₈in) wide paper together lengthways.

4 To link the daisies together to make a daisy chain, using a craft knife or scissors, cut a 1.5mm (¹⁄₁₆in) slit in the stem of one daisy partway down from the flower. Make a slit in the stem of another daisy in the same way. Insert the second stem through the slot in the first stem.

INSPIRATIONS

Flouncy flower tag
A single red frilly flower mounted onto a simple white tag makes a bold yet refined statement – perfect for a special birthday gift. A hole punched in the back panel is threaded with sheer pink ribbon to finish. The design could be adapted to make place cards for an anniversary dinner, or a similar bloom could be added to a hat shape (see pages 76–77) for a sophisticated card.

Daisy chain charmer
Here, four daisies with stems are made and linked together, as in the steps on the left, to create an attractive lattice-type arrangement. They are glued to pink card and mounted onto a paler pink folded card, the corners of both rounded to match. This card was designed as an artist trading card, which needs to measure 9 x 6.5cm (3¹⁄₂ x 2¹⁄₂in).

Looped leaves

Instead of making leaves from loose closed coils pinched into eye shapes, you can create more sinuously shaped leaves from looping paper strips by hand for an ornamental effect. The following instructions give you two alternative leaf designs, which can be used on their own (see Evergreen tag opposite) or in conjunction with any of the quilled flowers in this chapter.

You will need

• 3mm (⅛in) wide green paper
• Basic Tool Kit (see page 8)

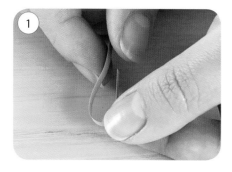

Form a loop in a 40cm (15¾in) length of the green paper about 3cm (1⅛in) high. Glue the end of the paper strip in place at the base of the loop.

Loop the free end of the paper strip over the first loop, making a slightly larger loop. Glue the loop in place at the base.

Repeat Step 2 to make a slightly larger loop than before and glue at the base. Either leave at three loops and trim the end of the paper or continue to create more loops.

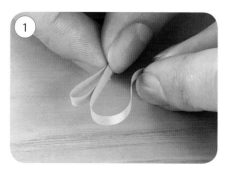

To make a side-looped leaf, again form a loop in a 40cm (15¾in) length of the green paper about 3cm (1⅛in) high and glue the end in place at the base. Make another, slightly larger loop to the side of the first loop and glue at the base.

Make a third loop to the side of the second loop, again slightly larger, and glue at the base. You can trim the end of the paper at this point and leave the leaf as is, without an outer wrapping, or continue on to the next step if you wish.

Take the free end of the paper around all three loops to encircle them, pulling the end of the paper quite tightly to hold the loops in place. Glue at the base and trim the excess paper.

TIP
These looped leaves could be used to create seaweed to accompany the beach items on pages 82–89.

Pretty petals

These highly attractive petals combine the standard coiling and pinching technique with hand looping, as featured in the leaves opposite, but in this case using ribbled or crimped paper (see page 10) in a graduated colour for an additional, easily achieved decorative effect.

You will need

• 3mm (⅛in) wide paper – graduated pink with dark centre, mauve
• ribbler (crimper)
• Basic Tool Kit (see page 8)

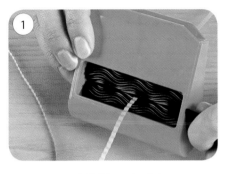

1

Insert a 30cm (12in) length of the graduated paper into the ribbler (crimper) and turn the handle so that the paper is pulled through and ribbled or crimped.

2

Make a loose closed coil with a 10cm (4in) length of the mauve paper, then pinch at one point to create a teardrop shape (see page 14). Cut the length of ribbled paper in half, then glue the pale end to the base of the teardrop.

TIP

If you don't have any suitable graduated paper, select a darker shade of mauve than that used for the teardrop coil for an alternative effective result.

4

Loop the ribbled paper around the teardrop twice more, making each loop slightly larger and gluing to secure each loop. Trim the end of the paper.

3

Loop the ribbled paper around the teardrop and glue the end to the other side of the base of the teardrop.

INSPIRATIONS

Evergreen tag

Underline the eco-friendly credentials of your gifts with this all-green foliage design, mounted onto complementary coloured purple paper and a darker purple rectangular card tag. The same design could be used to make invitations for an environmental fund-raising event or function with recycled paper and card.

Natural notepad

The looped and ribbled petals have been used here to create one whole flower and part of a flower for a corner motif as a decoration for this fridge notepad. The colour scheme can be adapted to coordinate with the recipient's kitchen décor. Alternatively, use the flowers to decorate greetings cards and gift tags.

47

Wonderful weddings

Quilling really comes into its own to mark such a big occasion, and a special hand-quilled wedding card and gift tag are sure to stand out and be noticed. You could also make the happy couple a unique framed design for a keepsake. And if you are feeling adventurous, why not create bespoke stationery for the day using the decorative motifs on offer here.

Wedding cake page 52

Precious rings page 53

Romantic rose page 50

Open heart page 51

Happy hearts

You can make quilled heart shapes in two ways, as demonstrated below, the first being the quickest and easiest method using a single loose closed coil and the second using two loose closed coils.

You will need

- 3mm (⅛in) wide paper – pink, red
- needle tool (optional)
- quilling board (optional)
- Basic Tool Kit (see page 8)

1

Make a loose closed coil from a 40cm (15¾in) length of the pink paper. Hold the coil in one hand and pinch at one point while simultaneously pushing inwards with a fingernail at the opposing point (see page 15). If you don't have good fingernails, use the tip of a needle tool. A quilling board can be used to ensure that the hearts are uniform in size, especially if you are making a batch.

1

Make two loose closed coils from 20cm (8in) lengths of the red paper. A quilling board can be used to ensure that the coils are all the same size, but this is optional – a heart with one side bigger than the other can look just as appealing.

2

Remove the coils from the quilling board, if using, and pinch into teardrops (see page 14). At this stage, note which side the inner parts of the coil spring to, then try to place the teardrops together so that the inner parts are facing inwards.

3

Glue the two teardrop shapes together by placing a small amount of glue along the two inner edges. Then apply glue on the underside of the heart and position on the card or other surface, holding and pinching in place while the glue dries.

TIP
Smaller hearts can be made in this way with shorter lengths of paper, but don't go too small, otherwise they will look less like hearts.

INSPIRATIONS

Heart hat-trick
Three hearts made from single pinched loose closed coils make a quick and easy design for this subtly ribbed pink gift tag. The scheme could be adapted to make multiple invitations or place cards for the big day.

Windows of the heart
For a simple yet elegant wedding card design, a row of three square apertures is cut in the front of a white single-fold card, then gold card glued to the inside of the card back, to which double-teardrop red hearts are mounted.

Romantic rose

This exquisite rose is possibly the hardest shape to make in quilling, as it requires a high degree of dexterity in folding the paper as well as concentration. But do persevere if you don't succeed after a couple of attempts, since the results – as you can see – are well worth the extra effort. It is best to use a long length of paper and then trim the end when the rose is the size you want; you can make tight rosebuds or full-sized blooms.

You will need

• 10mm (³⁄₈in) wide red paper
• 3mm (¹⁄₈in) wide green paper
• Basic Tool Kit (see page 8)

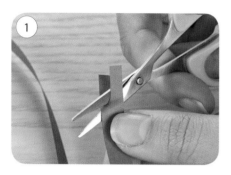

1 Take a 45cm (18in) length of the red paper and trim one end so that it is 2cm (³⁄₄in) long by 5mm (³⁄₁₆in) deep.

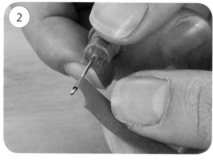

2 Insert the narrower end into the quilling tool and turn until the wider 10mm (³⁄₈in) width is reached.

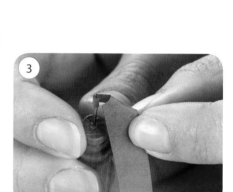

3 Fold the paper away from you, that is towards the tool, so that the paper is now at right angles to the tool.

TIP
For larger rose blooms, you may find it easier, after several turns, to remove the tool and continue folding just using your fingers.

4 Turn the quilling tool, lifting up the paper strip as you turn, so that it becomes horizontal again.

5 Make another fold, again at right angles in towards the tool, so that the paper hangs down, close to the previous fold. As you continue to fold and turn, space the folds out to make the gap between the previous fold and the next fold very slightly larger each time.

6 Once the rose is the size you want, trim the excess paper, fold the end inwards and glue in place. Before gluing, you can release the rose slightly to make it fuller. Turn the rose over and apply a generous amount of glue to the base. For the leaves, make teardrop shapes (see page 14) using different lengths of the green paper for a variation in size.

Open heart

This delicate heart uses the open coil technique to great effect, with the two coils made at either end of a centrally folded paper strip facing one another. Although it is quick to make, to ensure the best results, take time to adjust the coils before gluing so that they match.

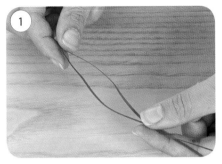

1 Fold a 40cm (15¾in) length of the red paper exactly in half.

2 Using the quilling tool, coil one end into the centre fold. Remove the tool and don't glue the coil at this stage.

3 Now use the tool to coil down to the centre fold from the other end and remove the tool. The coils may not be exactly the same size, but don't worry at this stage.

4 Place a dot of glue on the centre of each coil and very small dots around the edge of the coil and at the folded point. Position on your card or other surface, and before the glue dries, adjust the coils so that they are the same size.

TIP
Simply vary the length of the paper used to create open hearts of different sizes.

INSPIRATIONS

Favour flowers
This high-class favour box fashioned in the shape of a top hat is trimmed with a ribbon band and a posy of sumptuous quilled red roses interspersed with leaves.

Gorgeous in green
Roses need not be traditional pink and red, as these luscious green examples demonstrate. Use them to adorn a tag for a special wedding gift, as here, or for a place card; the colour can be changed to match any chosen scheme, such as apricot or yellow.

Positioned with perfection
A simple, single open heart makes a highly effective place card for the wedding breakfast, and is easy enough to make in quantity. Alternatively, use to decorate invitations or menu cards, or mount onto pink card for a tag.

51

Wedding cake

A three-tier wedding cake is a classic motif to mark the big occasion, and with quilling you can decorate it as elaborately as the real thing. Here, dusty pink paper edged with copper is used to catch the light and add sparkle and distinction to the design. The tiers are simply cut from card and mounted with adhesive foam pads to raise them to the same height as the quilled decorations.

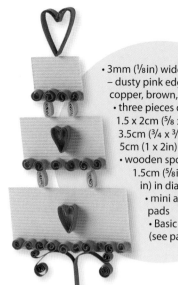

You will need

- 3mm (⅛in) wide paper – dusty pink edged with copper, brown, pale pink
- three pieces of pink card, 1.5 x 2cm (⅝ x ¾in), 2 x 3.5cm (¾ x ⅜in) and 2.5 x 5cm (1 x 2in)
- wooden spoons or dowel, 1.5cm (⅝in) and 1cm (⅜ in) in diameter
- mini adhesive foam pads
- Basic Tool Kit (see page 8)

For the top heart, wrap a 20cm (8in) length of the copper-edged pink paper around the larger wooden spoon handle or dowel, glue the end in place and remove (see Steps 1–2 opposite). Pinch at one point while pushing the opposing point inwards with your fingernail. Make two smaller hearts from 10cm (4in) lengths wrapped around the smaller wooden spoon handle or dowel.

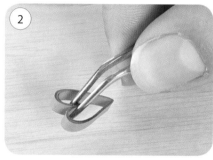

Place a small dot of glue in the top centre crease of each heart and a little on the underside of the crease (not the copper-edged side). Using tweezers, pinch the inner point and hold for a few seconds while the glue dries.

Make ten open 'S' coils with 4cm (1½in) lengths of the paper by coiling into the centre from one end inwards, then coiling from the other end outwards. Some scrolls are made with the copper edge in the tool up and some copper-edge down.

Using adhesive foam pads, mount the three pieces of pink card onto your chosen surface, ascending in size. Glue the scrolls along the bottom edges of each of the card pieces, inserting the quilling tool back into the centre of each scroll to help position it and recoil if necessary. Glue the large heart above the top tier and the two smaller hearts to the centre and bottom tiers.

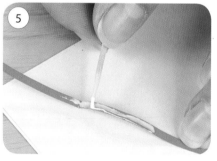

For the cake stand, fold a 10cm (4in) length of the brown paper in half, then open out and place on scrap paper. Apply glue for 3cm (1⅛in) to one side of the fold. Fold the paper over and press down so that the paper is glued double for 3cm (1⅛in) and the ends are free.

Using the quilling tool, coil each end outwards down to the glued section. Repeat to make a second coiled length, then glue together at the base. The tier posts are four 7cm (2¾in) lengths of pale pink paper formed into loose closed coils and pinched into rectangles (see page 15).

TIP
The wedding cake can be made entirely from white card and papers for a subtle, stylish effect.

Precious rings

These opulent, realistic-looking rings are quickly made by wrapping gold-edged paper around a wooden spoon handle or dowel, with a loose closed coil simply pinched into a square providing the decorative setting for a glued-on gem stone.

You will need
- 3mm (⅛in) wide gold-edged ivory paper
- clear gem stone
- wooden dowel or spoon
- superglue
- Basic Tool Kit (see page 8)

1

Wrap a 30cm (12in) length of the paper around the handle of a wooden spoon or dowel. Put a dot of glue on the end of the paper, wrap the paper around the handle, not too tightly, and press to the glue so that the rings of paper are exactly in line.

TIP

If you don't have a gem stone, add silver glitter glue to the top of the square coil or use gold Perfect Pearls™ (see page 59).

2

Continue to wind the paper around the handle until the end is reached. Remove and glue the end in place. If you have wrapped too tightly, you may not be able to remove it.

3

Make a loose closed coil with a 10cm (4in) length of the paper. Pinch into a square shape (see page 14) and glue to the ring at the join.

4

Pick up the gem stone with tweezers and place superglue on the underside, then position on the square coil.

INSPIRATIONS

Confection centrepiece

The fabulous quilled wedding cake takes centre stage in this memorable wedding card design, mounted onto a simple white single-fold card. The motif could also be used for a wedding album cover.

A gem of a card

This sparkling quilled ring set with a gem stone is presented to dramatic effect against a white panel framed with red mounted onto a pink card – a unique handmade design that the happy couple are sure to treasure. It could also be used to celebrate an engagement.

Forever together

Here, two rings, one with a gem stone, are symbolically combined and mounted onto a slightly ribbed pink card for a strong statement in every way. This could be used as a wedding gift tag as well as a place card.

Baby talk

The birth of a baby is such a special event that it demands to be marked in a memorable way, and quilling provides the perfect solution. In addition to the joyful parents' response, the effort involved in making unique christening or new baby cards, or even a captivating mobile, will be doubly rewarded in time when they are preserved as keepsakes.

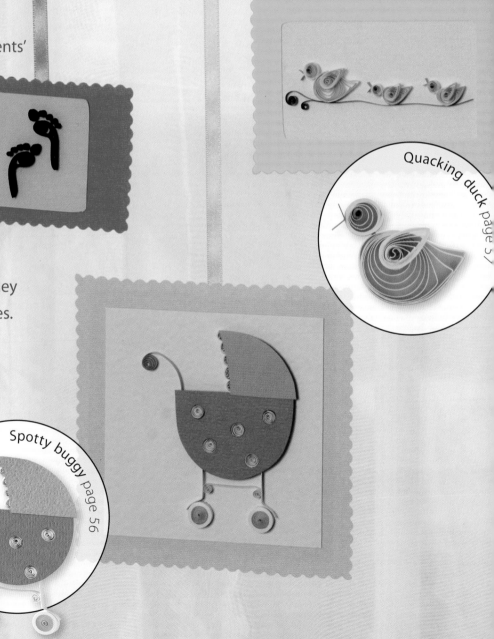

Quacking duck page 57

Spotty buggy page 56

Tiny feet

Baby feet are an enduring, endearing symbol of a newborn and are ideal for decorating all kinds of mementos of the happy event. Here, tiny quilled coils represent the toes and a bent teardrop-shaped loose closed coil forms the sole.

You will need
- 3mm (1/8in) wide blue or pink paper
- Basic Tool Kit (see page 8)

1 Make a loose closed coil from a 30cm (12in) length of the paper. Squeeze into an oval, then pinch halfway along one side and bend the end round. Apply glue to the underside and hold in place on the card or other surface you are decorating for a few seconds while the glue dries so that it holds its shape.

2 For the little toe, make a very tight coil with a 2cm (3/4in) length of the paper. While it is still on the quilling tool, add a tiny dot of glue on the end and press to the coil.

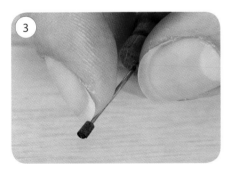

3 Use your fingernail to push the coil up and off the quilling tool.

4 Make the next two toes in the same way with 3cm (1 1/8in) lengths of the paper and the next toe with a 4cm (1 1/2in) length. Make the big toe with a 5cm (2in) length, but release it very slightly to make a looser coil. Assemble and glue in place. Repeat for the second foot.

TIP
The toes will fall off if not glued down properly, so rub your finger gently over them to check that they are properly secure.

INSPIRATIONS

Foot fest
For a cute christening or new baby card design, mount a pair of tiny feet on a pale blue-coloured panel, raised from a folded card with adhesive foam pads for extra impact. For a finishing flourish, cut two slits in the card front, thread with ribbon and tie in a dainty bow.

First footsteps
Here, pink baby feet made with metallic-pink edged paper were mounted onto pink card on a wooden block for a novel decoration – just the thing for a party in celebration of the new arrival. More blocks could be made with letters spelling out the baby's name (see page 104), or ducks (see page 57) or hearts in pastel colours (see page 49).

Spotty buggy

A pram or buggy is another timeless symbol for celebrating a newcomer to the family. The smart spots on this example are created by inserting quilled coils into holes punched in the card pram shape, which has been raised on adhesive foam pads so that the holes are recessed. The open coils simply unwind to fit the holes.

You will need
- pink card in two shades
- 3mm (⅛in) wide paper – white, pink
- 'anywhere' holepunch, 7mm (¼in) in diameter
- mini adhesive foam pads
- Basic Tool Kit (see page 8)

1

Using the templates on page 117, cut the pram body from one shade of pink card and the hood from the other. On the pram body, mark five equally spaced points with a pencil, then punch a hole at each pencil mark, holding the punch upside down to aid positioning.

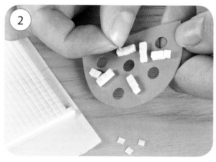

2

Place mini adhesive foam pads on one side of the pram body around the holes, but not too close to the edge. Remove the backing papers and press in position on your chosen surface.

3

Using a cocktail stick (toothpick), apply a dot of glue inside the punched holes on the surface below.

TIP

You can easily change the colour scheme to blue for a baby boy, or make two prams to celebrate a twin birth.

4

Make a loose coil from a 7cm (2¾in) length of the white paper and insert into a hole. Let the coil unravel in the hole.

5

Place adhesive foam pads on the underside of the pram hood and above the pram body as shown. Make five loose closed coils from 5cm (2in) lengths of white paper and pinch into crescent shapes (see page 14). Place glue on one side of each crescent and tuck under the side edge of the pram hood. Use a clean cocktail stick (toothpick) or tweezers to position the shapes accurately.

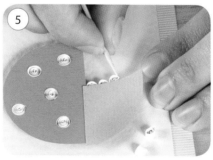

6

Glue a 40cm (15¾in) length of the white paper to 40cm (15¾in) of the pink and make a tight coil, starting with the pink. Repeat and position as wheels. Make pram legs from 2.5cm (1in) lengths of the white paper, curving the bottom ends for wheel arches and tucking the tops under the pram. Make an open coil in each end of a 7cm (2¾in) length of the white paper and glue between the legs. Make an open coil from a 10cm (4in) length of the pink paper and attach for the pram handle, tucking the end under the pram.

Quacking duck

This jolly little duck friend is quickly constructed from three coils, the two for the body and wing loosely coiled and pinched to shape. The head is formed from a strip of brown paper glued to a strip of yellow end to end and coiled so that the inner brown part forms the eye when pulled into position. The 'V'-shaped folded beak adds extra animation to the motif.

You will need

- 3mm (⅛in) wide paper – yellow, brown
- 2mm (¹⁄₁₆in) wide blue paper
- needle tool
- Basic Tool Kit (see page 8)

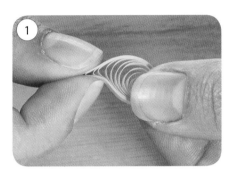

1

For the body, make a loose closed coil with a 40cm (15¾in) length of the yellow paper. Pull the centre to one side of the coil with your fingers, then pinch the other end and bend upwards to create a duck body shape. Glue to your chosen card or other surface.

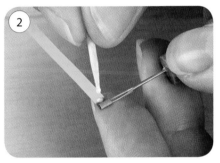

2

For the head, glue a 2cm (¾in) length of the brown paper to 15cm (6in) of the yellow end to end. Coil tightly, starting with the brown paper. When the yellow is reached, add a dot of glue, then continue coiling to make a loose closed coil.

3

Attach this coil to the card or other surface above the body, using the needle tool to pull the brown centre to one side of the head for the eye.

TIP

If you don't have a needle tool, insert a fine sewing needle into a dense wine cork.

4

For the beak, fold a 6mm (¼in) length of the brown paper in half and glue to the head at the fold. For the wing, make a loose closed coil with a 20cm (8in) length of yellow paper and pinch into a teardrop shape (see page 14). For water (see Ducks in a Row right), make an open coil in one end of a 10cm (4in) and a 5cm (2in) length of blue paper (see Step 4, page 95).

New baby onboard!
The posh-looking quilled buggy has been mounted onto pale pink card and then a darker pink folded card, with a strip of paper tied in a knot and attached to the spine side, for a fetching new baby or christening design.

Ducks in a row
For this cute duck family, add two ducklings to the duck made left by adjusting the paper measurements – 20cm (8in) for the body, 1cm (⅜in) brown and 7cm (2¾in) yellow for the head and 10cm (4in) for the wing. Mount onto pale yellow and then bright yellow card for a tag, with the addition of some yellow ribbon. This would also make an appropriate design for an Easter card.

Fairy fantasy

The fairy theme has an especially strong appeal for children and youngsters. But as well as providing them with enthralling designs for gifts and cards, it also offers them the ideal opportunity to try their hand at quilling, particularly as it involves using lots of colourful and glitzy paper and other fun materials.

Magic wand page 61

Fairy queen page 60

Fairy queen crown

This fairytale crown is easily made from pinched loose closed coils, topped with tight coil 'jewels' gilded with Perfect Pearls™ gold paint for light-catching lustre. Applying this paint is an effective alternative to using metallic-edged papers for the coils.

You will need

- 3mm (1/8in) wide paper – deep pink, pale pink
- gold Perfect Pearls™
- paintbrush
- saucer
- Basic Tool Kit (see page 8)

Make two loose closed coils with 20cm (8in) lengths of the deep pink paper and pinch into teardrop shapes (see page 14). Make another teardrop with a 30cm (12in) length and a rectangular shape with a 30cm (12in) length (see page 15).

TIP

You can use a gold pen instead of Perfect Pearls™, but it won't produce the same degree of sheen.

Glue the small teardrop shapes either side of the larger one onto card or another surface and the rectangular shape across the bottom. Make two tight coils with 5cm (2in) lengths of the pale pink paper and one tight coil from a 7cm (2¾in) length. Glue these above the points of the teardrops, the largest coil in the centre.

Tiara tag

Make a tag fit for a fairy princess's gift by mounting the pink crown onto a pale pink square of card and in turn onto a larger darker pink square, positioned diamond-style, punched and tied with pretty pink ribbon. The design could be used as name tags for personalizing party bags for a fairy-themed birthday party.

Place some of the gold Perfect Pearls™ on a clean saucer. Pick up a little water with a clean paintbrush and mix into the gold powder to make a thick liquid. If it is too runny, add more powder.

Paint the top edges of the round tight coils with the gold mixture. Alternatively, you can paint the whole of the coils.

Crown casket

This purple notepad holder has been magically transformed into a precious fairy casket with the addition of five sparkling crowns – two made with pink metallic-edged pink paper for the front and back and two with purple metallic-edged purple paper on the sides, all decorated with tight gold coils, plus a final variation in gold-edged ivory paper with pink and purple 'jewels' for the top. Ivory or gold tight coils on each corner add just the right finishing touch.

59

Fairy queen

Always a favourite with little girls, this unique quilled example uses different techniques for making and decorating the various components. The fairy's face is a tight closed coil coloured with pen and chalks, and the strands of hair are wound around a cocktail stick (toothpick) to curl, while looped strips give the wings a special airiness and glitter glue adds sparkle to her feet.

You will need

- 3mm (⅛in) wide paper – dark purple, ivory, very pale pink, yellow, pink, gold
- card – mauve, gold
- 10mm (⅜in) wide gold paper
- mini adhesive foam pads
- silver glitter glue
- pink chalk and applicator
- brown brush pen
- 2 wiggly eyes, 3mm (⅛in) in diameter
- superglue
- Basic Tool Kit (see page 8)

1

For the legs and feet, make two slightly loose closed coils by coiling 8cm (3⅛in) of 10cm (4in) lengths of the dark purple paper and gently pinch to make oval-type shapes. Glue to your chosen surface. Using the template on page 117, cut out the fairy body from mauve card. Attach mini adhesive foam pads to the underside. Mount overlapping the legs.

2

Apply dots of the glitter glue to the feet. Leave to dry.

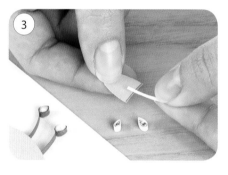

3

Using the template on page 117, cut out the arm from mauve card. Glue a strip of ivory paper 1.5mm x 1.5cm (1/16 x 5/8in) to the underside. Glue the arm to the body. For a hand, make loose closed coils with a 4cm (1½in) and a 3cm (1⅛in) length of ivory paper pinched into teardrops (see page 14). Glue either side of the end of the arm, the smaller shape uppermost.

TIP

You can turn the fairy queen into a Christmas fairy by using a red and green or silver and gold colour scheme.

4

Make the wings by forming four loops in a 25cm (10in) length of dark purple paper and three loops in a 20cm (8in) length, gluing at the base and trimming the ends (see page 46). Glue in position.

5

For the head, glue three 40cm (15¾in) lengths of the very pale pink paper end to end and make a very tight coil. Using an applicator, rub pink chalk onto the coil for cheeks, then add the wiggly eyes with superglue. Draw on a nose and mouth with a brown brush pen.

6

Cut lengths of the yellow paper into strands for hair and glue to the head. Use a clean cocktail stick (toothpick) to curl them. Attach the head to the body. Make a crown following the instructions on page 59 but without the 'jewels' and glue in place. Make a wand from gold card and paper following the instructions opposite but without the frilled centre and attach in position with mini adhesive foam pads.

Magic wand

Go to town with this fabulous star-shaped fairy wand, complete with gold coiled streamers. Its wonderfully tactile central decoration is made using the fringing technique, as in the Frilly Flower, page 44, but without the central coil, for a pompom-type effect.

You will need

- 10mm (³/₈in) wide gold paper
- deep pink card
- 90 degree-angled fringing tool
- small star punch
- 'anywhere' holepunch, 7mm (¹/₄in) in diameter
- mini adhesive foam pads
- Basic Tool Kit (see page 8)

1

Insert a 15cm (6in) length of the gold paper into the fringing tool, then move the handle up and down to fringe the paper. Make a tight closed coil from the fringed paper and glue the end in place.

2

Punch a star shape from the pink card. Mark the centre of the star with a pencil, then punch a hole at the mark with the 'anywhere' holepunch.

3

Mount the star onto your card or other surface with mini adhesive foam pads. Place glue all over the base of the fringed coil and insert into the hole in the star. Press down, then spread the fringe out.

4

Glue two 7cm (2³/₄in) lengths of the gold paper together lengthways and trim to taper at one end. Cut thin strands of the gold paper 2mm (¹/₁₆in) wide, then cut into two sets consisting of a 3cm (1¹/₈in), 4cm (1¹/₂in) and 5cm (2in) length. Glue each set of lengths together at one end, then coil the other ends in different directions without gluing. Tuck each set under the pink star either side of the stick and glue in place.

TIP

The paper used here is gold on both sides, but you can use paper that is gold on one side only you if wish.

In-flight fairy

The quilled fairy queen has been given due prominence in this enchanting design, mounted 'mid-air' on a cream background attached to a pink square card. This would make a delightful card for a young girl's birthday.

Spell bound

Bring more than a touch of magic and mystery to a shocking pink spiral-bound notebook by mounting the fairy wand on the cover, positioned breaking out of a pale pink panel for an added sense of drama – an ideal place for storing away all those special secrets and spells.

Animal magic

Animals make ever-popular subjects for cards and gifts, and are surprisingly easy to capture in quilling form. Here you will see how loose closed coils can be pinched, bent and otherwise manipulated into various characteristic body and head shapes, both in profile and face on, then brought to life with added details, such as wiggly eyes, curled tails and spiky whiskers.

Pooch's paw print see page 67

Friendly dog page 66

Black cat page 64

Feline's fishbone page 65

Mini mouse

Scampering mice make very cute quilled decorations whether in brown or white and are easily constructed from triangular pinched coils for the large pink-centred ears resting on a pinched teardrop for the body. The strip for the tail can be curled with your fingernail in different endearing ways. The pink tight coil nose and whiskers make the mice look as though they are nibbling away.

- 3mm (⅛in) wide paper – brown, pink
- 2mm (¹⁄₁₆in) wide brown paper
- wiggly eye, 3mm (⅛in) in diameter
- superglue
- Basic Tool Kit (see page 8)

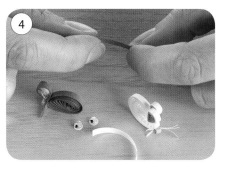

For the whiskers, cut a 1.5cm (⅝in) length of the 2mm (¹⁄₁₆in) wide brown paper into three fine strands at either end, with the centre left uncut. Attach to the pointed end of the mouse body. Make a tight coil from a 5cm (2in) length of the pink paper and glue over the centre of the whisker strip for a nose.

Taper a 5cm (2in) length of the 3mm (⅛in) wide brown paper to a point for the tail and curl with your fingernail. Attach to the body. Add a wiggly eye to the head with superglue. For a white mouse, substitute the same widths of white paper for the brown papers used in the instructions above.

TIP
A sturdier mouse could be made using 5mm (³⁄₁₆in) wide papers.

INSPIRATIONS

Magician's assistants

A magician's key prop – a top hat – is decorated with his essential accomplices – three white mice – to make a fabulous favour box for a children's birthday party or for a Harry Potter-style magic show. The hat could also house some special sweets or little party playthings to add to the fun.

Artist's apprentice

This tiny quilled mouse looks like he is running along the pencil – and what a surprise that will be for the lucky recipient! But fun-loving, artistic friends and family are sure to be delighted by such a gift. You could attach the pencil and mouse to a diary or sketchpad.

Black cat

Any shape can be created with quilling and can be used as a way of animating a motif, as with this cat, where a loose closed coil for its body has been curled into an arched shape so that it looks poised to jump, pounce or stretch. The tight coil yellow eyes with a black centre have a characteristically feline stare.

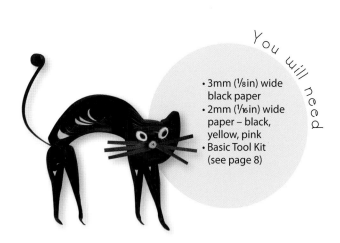

You will need

• 3mm (⅛in) wide black paper
• 2mm (¹⁄₁₆in) wide paper – black, yellow, pink
• Basic Tool Kit (see page 8)

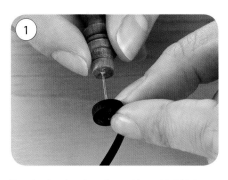

For the body, glue three 40cm (15¾in) lengths of the 3mm (⅛in) wide black paper together end to end. Use to make a loose closed coil and glue to your chosen surface in an arched shape.

TIP

You can easily alter the body shape and legs of the cat so that it is jumping or stretching. Or adapt the dog project (see page 66) to make a sitting cat.

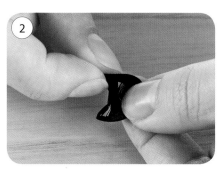

For the head, glue two 40cm (15¾in) lengths of the 3mm (⅛in) wide black paper together end to end. Use to make a loose closed coil. Pinch at one point, then at the same point on the other side of the coil to make ears.

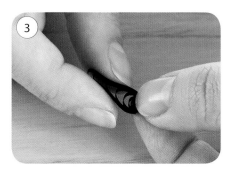

For the legs, make four very loose closed coils from 20cm (8in) lengths of the 3mm (⅛in) wide black paper, then pinch almost flat at one end to a point.

For the eyes, glue 1cm (⅜in) of 2mm (¹⁄₁₆in) wide black paper to 1cm (⅜in) of the yellow paper end to end. Make a tight coil, starting from the black paper. Glue the end in place and pinch flat. For the nose, make a tight coil with a 1.5cm (⅝in) length of the pink paper. Cut fine strands of black paper for whiskers.

In order to maintain the shape of the leg, use a cocktail stick (toothpick) to place glue inside the flat end of the coil, then press together, leaving the rounded end unglued. Bend the pointed end of the shape slightly for a paw effect.

Glue the four legs to the body. Glue the features to the head, then glue over the body and front two legs. For the tail, coil a 10cm (4in) length of the 3mm (⅛in) wide black paper for about 6cm (2⅜in), then release the coil slightly and glue in place. Glue to the cat.

Feline's fishbone

This bleached white fishbone is best set off by a dark background. The thin paper is ideal for re-creating the fineness of the bones, and cutting out the centre of the coiled head enhances the stark skeletal effect.

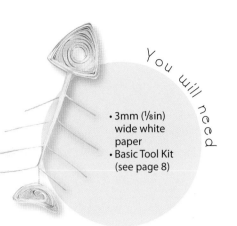

You will need
- 3mm (⅛in) wide white paper
- Basic Tool Kit (see page 8)

1 For the head, make a loose closed coil with a 20cm (8in) length of the white paper. Pinch into a triangular shape (see page 14).

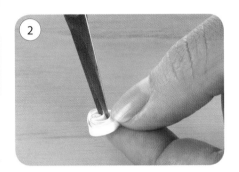

2 Using scissors, cut out the centre of the coil. For the tailbone, make a loose closed coil with a 15cm (6in) length of the white paper and pinch into a crescent shape (see page 14). Glue to the card or other surface at a distance from the head.

3 Cut nine 3.5cm (1⅜in) lengths of white paper. Glue pieces either side of one piece for the backbone, applying glue to 3cm (1⅛in) of the lengths nearest the tail, then 2.5cm (1in) for the middle lengths and 2cm (¾in) for those closest to the head. Bend at an angle to the backbone.

4 Glue the bones to the card or other surface between the head and the tailbone, placing glue only along the underside of the backbone. Trim the ends of the side bones so that they are even on each side and form a skeleton shape.

TIP
A row of these fishbones under or around a quilled cat would make an eye-catching border.

INSPIRATIONS

Spooked cat card
The haunted-looking black cat makes the perfect image for an invitation to a Halloween party, spotlighted in a vibrant orange circle mounted onto a red folded card. A length of ribbon tied in a bow around the base of the card adds a softening touch.

Tell-tail tag
Set against dark blue card for maximum impact, the fishbone makes a fun feature for a gift tag, which is sure to amuse any cat lover. You could use it to present a special treat for their feline friend.

65

Friendly dog

As opposed to the cat that is pictured in profile, this equally lively dog is sitting face on as if expecting a walk. He is simply constructed from a series of loose closed coils, with the forelegs forming a second layer for extra dimension. The curled pink tongue and flattened coil wagging tail add further to his personality.

You will need

• 3mm (⅛in) wide paper – pale brown, dark brown, black, white, pink
• 1.5mm (¹⁄₁₆in) wide gold-edged ivory paper
• Basic Tool Kit (see page 8)

1 For the dog's head, make a loose closed coil with a 40cm (15¾in) length of the pale brown paper. Glue to card or another surface. For the ears, glue a 10cm (4in) length of the pale brown paper to a 10cm (4in) length of the dark brown end to end and make a loose closed coil, starting with the dark brown. Repeat and pinch into teardrop shapes (see page 14). Glue either side of the head.

2 For the body, glue two 40cm (15¾in) lengths of the pale brown paper together end to end and make a loose closed coil. For the legs, make loose coils with a 20cm (8in) length of the same paper and pinch into teardrop shapes. Glue in place.

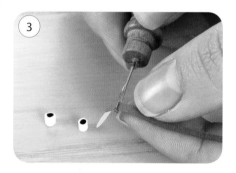

3 For the eyes, glue a 1cm (⅜in) length of the black paper to 3.5cm (1⅜in) of the white end to end and make a tight coil, starting with the black. Repeat. Glue inside the head. For the mouth and tongue, glue a tiny piece of pink paper to one end of a 5cm (2in) length of the dark brown paper. Make a loose closed coil, leaving the tongue hanging down, and pinch flat.

4 Insert the mouth and tongue into the head – you may need to use tweezers to move the coil about to make room.

TIP
You could add wiggly eyes for an extra dimension of animation.

5 For the paws, make six loose closed coils from 4cm (1½in) lengths of the dark brown paper, then pinch into teardrops and glue into two groups of three. For the forelegs, glue a 10cm (4in) length of the pale brown to a 10cm (4in) length of the dark brown paper and make a loose closed coil, starting with the dark brown. Repeat. Glue in place.

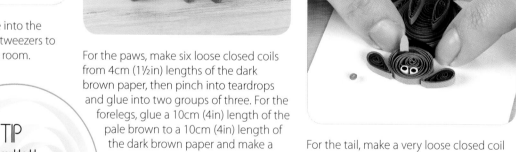

6 For the tail, make a very loose closed coil with a 20cm (8in) length of the dark brown paper and pinch almost flat. For the collar, make a small fold at either end of a 2cm (¾in) length of the black paper. Glue one end around the neck, then the other end, holding in place while the glue dries. For a tag, make a tight coil with a 1.5cm (⅝in) length of the gold-edged ivory paper.

Pooch's paw prints and bone

Quilled shapes don't always need to be joined together to make an effective motif, such as these paw prints, made from just four separate coils, which are really quick to make. The bone consists of two pinched coils linked by a central strip of paper folded over several times.

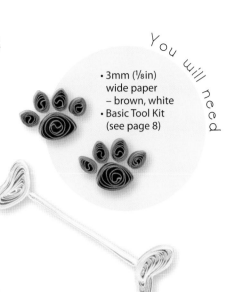

You will need

- 3mm (⅛in) wide paper – brown, white
- Basic Tool Kit (see page 8)

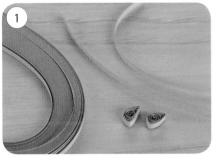

1

For the paw prints, for each one, make a loose closed coil with a 10cm (4in) length of the brown paper and pinch into a crescent shape (see page 14).

2

Make four loose closed coils per paw print with 5cm (2in) lengths of the brown paper; vary the size by allowing some coils to release slightly more before gluing. Pinch into teardrop shapes (see page 14). Glue the crescents onto the card or other surface. Glue the larger teardrops at the centres of the crescents, with two smaller ones either side.

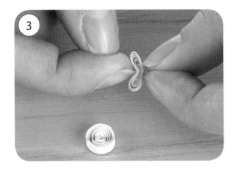

3

For the bone, make a loose closed coil from a 20cm (8in) length of the white paper and pinch into a crescent shape.

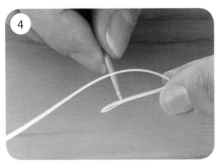

4

Take a 20cm (8in) length of the white paper, fold over 2.5cm (1in) at one end and glue in place. Continue folding over in the same way and gluing each time. Glue one crescent shape to the card or other surface, then the central bone and finally the other crescent shape.

TIP
Instead of dog paw prints, you can change the size, colour and number of toes to make other animal footprints.

INSPIRATIONS

Top dog bookmark
The waggy dog is mounted onto a white card doorway attached to a kennel-shaped piece of brown card, which is glued to a rectangular piece of brown card for a bookmark. Two slits cut in the base enable him to sit obediently on top of the page to encourage young readers.

Canine call signs
Here, the doggy paw prints and bone have been combined to make a novelty gift tag to bring a smile to the face of any dog lover. These quirky motifs could also be used to decorate a photo frame for a portrait of a beloved canine companion or a memo pad or notebook.

Oriental style

Oriental-inspired designs have a delicate, decorative quality that brings a sophistication and distinction to papercrafted items. Quilling, with its flowing lines and fine, intricate forms, lends itself particularly well to this style, especially when produced in soft, harmonious hues of orange, pink and red.

Lucky lantern *page 70*

Beautiful bloc

Exotic bamboo *page 71*

Exquisite flower *page 73*

Ornamental fan

To embellish this elegant Far Eastern-inspired fan, tight coils have been made with a needle tool so that they have open centres, then flowing movement introduced by winding a double length of darker paper around the coils. Using metallic-edged papers adds overall richness to the design.

You will need

- 3mm (⅛in) wide paper – copper-edged ivory, gold-edged brown
- card – orange, brown
- needle tool
- Basic Tool Kit (see page 8)

1 Place a 5cm (2in) length of the copper-edged ivory paper around a needle tool.

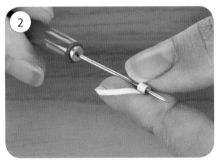

2 Hold the needle tool still in one hand and wrap the paper around the tool with the other hand, making a tight coil. Glue the end in place and remove the tool. Make three coils each with 5cm (2in), 4cm (1½in) and 3cm (1⅛in) lengths of the paper.

3 Using the templates on page 117, cut out the fan shape from orange card and the handle from brown card. Glue the coils to the fan in groups of three at evenly spaced intervals. Glue the handle to the bottom of the fan.

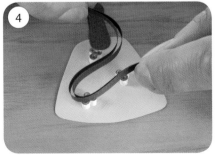

4 Apply glue to the upper side of the top coils in each group. Fold a 20cm (8in) length of the gold-edged brown paper in half and glue the ends together. Bend around the coils and press to the glued sides to secure.

Fridge fan

Make a single ornamental fan into a distinctive fridge magnet by gluing a magnet to the reverse side. You could also turn it into a fabulous gift tag for an oriental-style present by mounting it onto a piece of complementary coloured card, punching a hole through the card and threading with cord or ribbon.

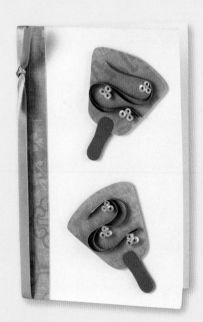

Fan fantasy

Two fans are used here to create an elegant card design to celebrate a birthday or an anniversary. The main fan shapes were cut from oriental-style printed paper, with the same paper used for a decorative border for the card spine, further embellished with coordinating ribbon tied in a knot. The fans were attached to the pale orange card with adhesive foam pads for added depth.

Lucky lantern

This traditional oriental-style lantern is ingeniously made by pinching four loose closed coils, then gluing them together in graduating shades. The shapes hang free to allow daylight to illuminate the quilling effect. A quilling board is used here to ensure that the coils are uniform in size before being pinched so that they exactly match.

You will need

- 3mm (⅛in) wide paper in shades of red and orange
- quilling board
- Basic Tool Kit (see page 8)

Make a loose closed coil with a 40cm (15¾in) length of red paper. Add a dot of glue to the end of the paper with a cocktail stick (toothpick).

TIP

Take care when handling these coils, otherwise the centres will pop out. You can apply glue to the reverse side of the lantern to help keep the centres in position.

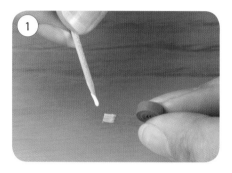

Place the coil in a circle template about 2cm (¾in) in diameter in the quilling board. Allow the coil to release to the edges of the template, then make sure that the end of the paper is glued in place. Make three more coils in this way from the different shades of paper, graduating from red to orange.

Using your fingertips, pinch two opposite sides of each coil to form a teardrop shape (see page 14).

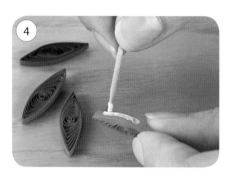

Using a cocktail stick (toothpick), apply glue along the edge of one side of the darkest-coloured teardrop shape, but not right to the points, then adhere to the next darkest teardrop shape.

Adhere the remaining teardrop shapes in the same way, with the palest coloured at the bottom. Hold the shapes together for a few seconds while the glue dries.

Fold a 2cm (¾in) length of pale orange paper over to make a loop and glue to the top of the lantern (the darkest-coloured teardrop shape). Glue a 1.5cm (⅝in) length of pale orange paper, snipped into about four strands, to the bottom of the lantern.

Exotic bamboo

This highly attractive and versatile quilled motif is a great way to start making and using pinched shapes, since in this instance they don't need to be uniform in shape to create the desired natural effect. Some of the leaves are layered on top of each other to add extra dimensional interest.

You will need

- 3mm (⅛in) wide papers – green, brown
- Basic Tool Kit (see page 8)

For the leaves, cut several lengths of the green paper, varying between 15cm (6in) and 20cm (8in) long. Make loose closed coils with each length. Pinch one side of each coil very tightly and gently pinch the opposite side to flatten the coil, then pinch inwards to bend the tightly pinched end. Set aside.

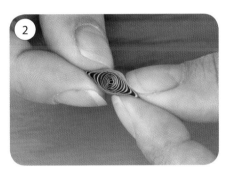

Make a loose closed coil with a 20cm (8in) length of the brown paper. Pinch at two opposing points to form an eye shape (see page 14).

TIP
You can make a larger bamboo stem and leaves by simply doubling the lengths of paper used to make the loose closed coils.

Push the shape inwards at the pinched ends and pinch again to form an irregular rectangular shape. Make several shapes in the same way. Glue some of the shapes end to end to your chosen surface to form a curved stem, leaving a small gap between each shape, adding other shapes here and there as side branches. Glue the leaf shapes around the stem, making a double layer at the top and the ends of the branches.

INSPIRATIONS

Lantern window
Strung onto paper cord, this trio of lanterns hangs in an upright aperture cut in a single-fold orange card, with a piece of paler orange card attached to the back panel of the card behind it, thereby allowing the light to shine through the coils. This would be ideal for a Chinese New Year card or an invitation to a special-occasion oriental meal.

Bamboo breezer
Here, a curved stem of bamboo, as if bending in a breeze, is attached to a vibrant yellow, upright-shaped folded card. This design would delight a gardener with a penchant for tropical plants or those moving or travelling to an exotic location. It would also help to make the message 'remember to water my plants while I'm away' especially memorable!

Beautiful bloom

This elaborate, double-layered flower is made using a special technique in which punched heart-shaped petals are precisely positioned and glued to paper and then coiled and fanned out. The translucent paper for the petals captures that essential delicate oriental quality.

- orange translucent paper
- clear parchment or translucent paper
- 3mm (⅛in) wide paper – pale cream, deep pink, orange
- heart punch
- pale gold 3-D paint
- Basic Tool Kit (see page 8)

Punch six heart shapes from orange translucent paper and eight from clear parchment or translucent paper.

TIP

The spacing of the punched shapes is crucial in creating a successful flower with this technique, so be sure to follow the instructions carefully.

Glue a 10cm (4in) length of the pale cream paper to 15cm (6in) of the pink end to end. Then glue the end of the pink paper to a 30cm (12in) length of the 3mm (⅛in) orange paper. Cut four narrow strands of the pink paper 1cm (⅜in) in length and glue to the end of the pale cream paper for stamens.

Place the strip of joined papers on scrap paper and glue the six orange hearts where the pale cream joins the pink paper. Allow a 2mm (¹⁄₁₆in) gap between the base of each heart. Glue the tips of the hearts about halfway across the paper strip.

Glue the eight parchment or translucent hearts onto the strip 5cm (2in) along from the orange hearts in the same way.

Place the end with the stamens into the quilling tool, ensuring that the hearts are facing away from the quilling tool. Make a tight coil and glue the end in place.

Use your fingers to fan out the hearts. Add dots of gold 3-D paint onto the ends of the stamens and leave to dry.

Exquisite flower

This is a quicker version of the double flower opposite, using only four petals, punched with a circle punch, and without stamens. Again, translucent paper is used for the petals, and grouped together these blooms make a beautiful display.

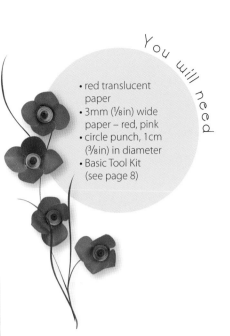

You will need

- red translucent paper
- 3mm (⅛in) wide paper – red, pink
- circle punch, 1cm (⅜in) in diameter
- Basic Tool Kit (see page 8)

Using the circle punch, punch four circles from the red translucent paper.

Glue a 5cm (2in) length of the 3mm (⅛in) red paper to 20cm (8in) of the pink end to end, then glue the end of the pink to 15cm (6in) of the 3mm (⅛in) red. Glue the punched shapes at the join of the pink and longer length of red paper. The circles will need to overlap and glue halfway across the paper strip.

Make a tight coil, starting with the shorter length of red paper, and then glue the end in place; the glue must be dry before coiling, otherwise the circles will fall out.

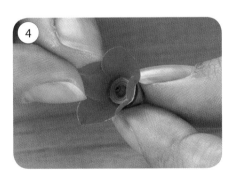

Fan the circles out and then pinch to form petal shapes. Leave some slightly closed and fan out the others more to give them a natural-looking variation.

TIP

If at Step 3 you can tell that the petals are not positioned correctly, don't glue the end but use this as a reference for the next flower.

INSPIRATIONS

Floating flower tag

To create a sumptuous gift tag, mount the open flower head onto a circle of pinky orange card, then a larger circle of orange card, and add a matching ribbon tie. You could also make this into a stunning brooch, presented on a card for a special summertime gift. Or several flower heads could be mounted onto a wire ring for a celebration cake decoration.

Floral frame

Here, a functional magnetic fridge notepad has been transformed into a glamorous gift, decorated with a sinuous spray of the small, delicate red flowers. These have been glued to either side of three red stems, with strands of paper tapered at one end emanating from the main stem.

73

Fab Fashion

Fashion is a subject close to many people's hearts and re-creating those defining accessories in quilling will add great entertainment value to your greetings cards and gifts. In the same way that fashion caters for all ages and tastes, here you will find something for everyone, from sophisticated hats for discerning ladies to mini pots of nail varnish for aspirational tweenies.

Funky phone page 81

Chic shoe page 78

Trendy bag page 79

Feathered hat page 77

Tendril-trimmed hat page 76

Magic make-up page 80

Tendril-trimmed hat

This classic Parisian fashion house hat will add a touch of class to any gift card or tag. It is adorned with an opulent trimming of open spiral coils made from two-tone quilling papers (see page 7), which graduate from pale to dark to pale again along the length of each strip, so that the strongest colour is concentrated in the centre.

You will need

- 3mm (⅛in) wide pink with dark centre graduated paper
- red card
- Basic Tool Kit (see page 8)

Coil a 14cm (5½in) length of the paper towards the centre of the strip for about 6cm (2⅜in), then release the coil without gluing. Coil the other end towards the centre until you almost meet the other coil and release. Repeat with five more strips. You can make some into 'S'-shaped scrolls (see Step 3, page 52).

Place a small amount of glue on the centre of one coiled strip and glue the centre of another coiled strip to it. Glue another to the other side of the first in the same way. Glue the remaining coiled strips in the same way to either side of the joined coiled strips.

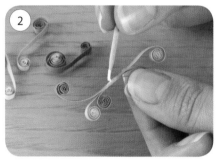

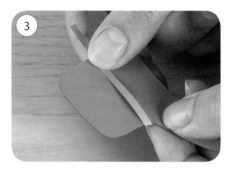

Using the template on page 118, cut out the hat shape from red card. Attach a strip of the pink paper around the base of the hat crown for a hat band, folding the ends around the sides of the hat.

TIP

This hat offers the perfect opportunity to use up those tiny bits of paper left over from other projects to make the open spiral coils.

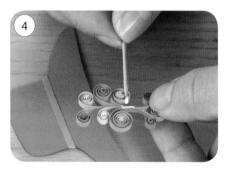

Place a small dot of glue in the centre of the joined-together coiled strips and attach to the pink hat band to one side of the hat.

Glue the hat to your chosen card or other surface. Make a tight closed coil from a 10cm (4in) length of the pink paper and glue to the centre of the joined-together coiled strips.

Feathered hat

This ultra-modish hat takes its inspiration from those high-society horserace-goers in their top designer garb, so it is guaranteed to bring a unique sense of style to your cards, gift packages or party invitations. The feathers are fashioned from fringed, graduated-coloured paper strips, where the strongest colour at one end fades to white at the other.

- 10mm (⅜in) wide purple graduated paper
- purple card
- 45 degree-angled fringing tool
- Basic Tool Kit (see page 8)

1 Fold a 10cm (4in) length of the purple paper in half along its length.

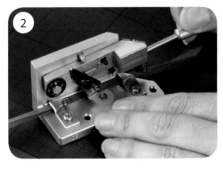

2 Insert it into the fringing tool with the fold at the back, against the vertical part of the tool. Move the handle up and down to fringe the paper. Remove the paper and check that there are no uncut parts.

3 Cut a 2.5cm (1in) piece of the fringed paper, then trim each side to form an oval or feather shape. Repeat to make about five feathers. Cut an unfringed, pale piece of the purple paper lengthways into the same quantity of narrow strips 7cm (2¾in) in length. Using the template on page 118, cut two hat shapes from purple card. Glue a narrow strip of pale purple paper to the base of the crown of one, folding the ends around the sides, then glue the two hats together. Glue the feathers to the strips and attach to the hat, trimming the ends as required.

TIP
If you don't have any graduated paper, use various shades of purple for an equally effective result.

Magnetic attraction
Simply glue a small magnet to the back of this gorgeous accessory to make a fridge magnet for your favourite fashionista – just the thing for keeping those shopping lists of designer goods to hand. Alternatively, use it to decorate a gift box made in the style of a hatbox, for an especially luxurious present.

Crowning glory
Here, a hat shape cut from pale purple card has been mounted onto a square red folded card, then embellished with feathers cut from three different shades of purple paper, trimmed with tumbling pink spirals. This would make an ideal Mother's Day card, mother-of-the-bride thank you card or an upmarket invitation to the races or a shopping trip.

Chic shoe

The flamboyant decoration for this cutting-edge fashion shoe is made using the Spreuer technique (see page 17), as developed by leading quiller Jane Jenkins, taking inspiration from corn dolly maker's in Switzerland who made shapes from flattened straw on a wide-toothed comb. Here instead, paper strips are threaded around and through the widely spaced prongs of an onion holder.

You will need
- 3mm (⅛in) wide two-tone pink paper
- card – cream, pink
- 5mm (³⁄₁₆in) wide pink paper
- onion holder
- adhesive foam pad
- Basic Tool Kit (see page 8)

Fold 3mm (⅛in) over one end of a length (44cm/17¼in) of the two-tone paper and loop under the first rung of the onion holder, with the bright pink colour facing up. Place a dot of glue on the folded-over end on the bright pink side. Holding this end in place with your fingers, take the other end up to rung 10 and thread in between rung 10 and rung 11. Pull the paper through and press onto the folded-over end. This is the centre loop.

Take the end of the paper up to rung 8, thread between rung 8 and rung 9, then pull through.

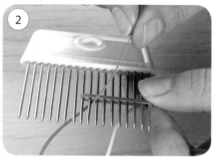

Cross the paper over the centre loop to rung 3 and thread between rung 3 and 4, then pull through. Cross the paper over at the back and take it up to rung 8 on the other side of the centre loop. Thread through and back down over the centre loop to rung 3.

TIP

To save having to count up the number of rungs, place a strip of masking tape along the plastic edge of the onion holder and use a pen to number each rung consecutively.

Take the paper up to rung 7, cross over down to rung 4, then cross over at the back up to rung 7 on the other side of the centre loop.

Wrap the end of the paper around the shape in the centre, through the centre rung, and trim. Using the templates on page 118, cut out a shoe sole from cream card and an upper from pink card. Attach an adhesive foam pad to the underside of the upper to raise it slightly, then glue to the sole around the outer edge only.

Carefully slide the Spreuer decoration from the onion holder and glue to the shoe upper. To add a heel, make a loose closed coil from a 20cm (8in) length of the 5mm (³⁄₁₆in) wide pink paper and glue to the underside of the sole.

Trendy bag

Even in its simplest form, quilling can add decorative detail to any motif, such as this smart fashion accessory, to give it that special finishing touch. Here, four off-centred, also known as 'eccentric', coils are grouped around a shiny brad for a designer look to rival Chanel or Dior!

You will need

- 2mm (1/16in) wide purple paper
- green card
- silver pen
- silver-edged pearl brad
- quilling board and pins
- Basic Tool Kit (see page 8)

1
Make a coil with a 20cm (8in) length of the purple paper. Apply glue to the end, then insert the coil into the 1cm (3/8in) diameter template in the quilling board. Let the coil release to fit the circle. Make three more identical coils.

2
Use a pin to bring the centre of the first coil to the edge where the paper join is. Then press the pin into the board. Repeat for the other coils.

3
Place a dot of glue near the pin where the centre of the coil has been pulled over in order to hold it in place. Leave the glued coils in the quilling board to dry while cutting the handbag.

4
Using the template on page 118, cut a handbag from green card. Using the silver pen, draw rows of stitching around the handle and down each side, and add two parallel lines at the bag top as shown. Insert the brad into the centre of the bag and bend the 'wings' to flatten on the reverse. Glue the four coils around the brad, with the centres nearest to the brad.

INSPIRATIONS

Retail therapy
This card captures that thrill of opening a box of brand-new shoes, nestling alluringly on a bed of tissue paper. An appropriate greeting could be added to the upper sole where the maker's label would be on a real pair of shoes, or add the name of the recipient's favourite fashion designer.

Designer bag tag
Turn the bag into a tag for a fashion trendsetter by knotting two lengths of ribbon in different colours together to the handle; you will need to back the bag with a second piece of card to cover the 'wings' of the brad. It would also make a great motif for a young teenager's birthday card.

Magic make-up

A range of coordinating nail varnish and lipstick colours is a must-have in any self-respecting fashion follower's everyday kit, and these upmarket-looking examples are craftily created entirely from paper. The nail varnish bottles consist of just two tight coils, one in a mauve shade for the base and the other in gold for the top. Since wider paper strips are unwieldy to coil using a quilling tool, the lipstick base is coiled around a cocktail stick (toothpick), with a pinched loose closed coil for the lipstick itself.

You will need

• 10mm (³⁄₈in) wide paper – shades of purple, gold
• sheet of purple paper
• 5mm (³⁄₁₆in) wide gold paper
• 3mm (¹⁄₈in) wide red paper
• gold pen
• Basic Tool Kit (see page 8)

For the nail varnish, make a tight coil with a 40cm (15¾in) length of one shade of purple paper, then make a tight coil with a 30cm (12in) length of the 10mm (³⁄₈in) gold paper. The gold paper does not glue very easily, so you need to hold for a few more seconds than with other papers.

Using the gold pen, draw a band around the base of the purple coil. Add suitable words to the side of the coil; I used squiggles to give the impression of text.

TIP
When using different shades of paper, you may find that they are different thicknesses, so even if you use exactly the same lengths of each paper, the coils may vary slightly in size.

Glue the gold coil to the top of the purple coil and hold in place for a few seconds. Make additional bottles of nail varnish using the other purple shades of paper.

For the lipstick bases, place the sheet of purple paper on a cutting mat and use a metal ruler with a cork base to cut several strips 1.3 x 20cm (½ x 8in).

Coil one strip around a clean cocktail stick (toothpick). Glue the end in place and remove the stick. Draw a gold band around the base of the coil with the pen. For the lid, make a tight coil with a 40cm (15¾in) length of a matching shade of purple paper and add a gold band.

Make a tight coil with a 12cm (4¾in) length of the 5mm (³⁄₁₆in) wide gold paper. Glue to the top of the base. Make a loose closed coil with a 7cm (2¾in) length of the red paper. Pinch into a lipstick shape and glue to the gold coil. Make additional lipsticks in the same way with the remaining purple strips.

Funky phone

A cutting-edge mobile (cell) phone is the party-goer's essential accessory, for the young or grown-up, so indulge their designer aspirations with this innovative (and inexpensive) paper example. Using pink paper edged with metallic pink adds contemporary-style glitz to the quilled elements.

You will need

- 3mm (⅛in) wide metallic pink-edged pink paper
- pink card
- pink gel pen
- silver stickers – numbers 1–9, 2 stars, cross, square
- clear dome sticker
- photo
- Basic Tool Kit (see page 8)

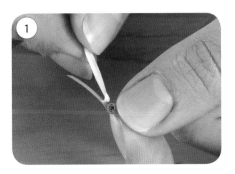

1

To make a single musical note, tightly coil a 5cm (2in) length of the pink paper for 4cm (1½in). Remove the tool and glue the end in place. Leave the tail as it is or bend the top over.

2

For the double notes, take a 10cm (4in) length of the pink paper and make two folds 4.5cm (1¾in) from either end.

TIP
Instead of a photo, you could write a text message.

4

Cut a long rectangular shape from pink card. Using the pink gel pen, draw a grid of nine boxes for the keypad. Add a silver number sticker to each box. Add two stars, a cross and a square sticker above the numbers. Place a clear dome sticker over the area of the photo that you want to use, then trim around the edge. Glue to the top of the phone. Glue the phone to your chosen surface, with the notes arranged either side.

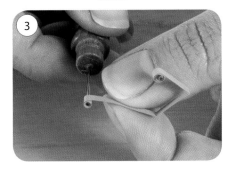

3

Make a tight coil in one end and glue in place. Coil the other end in the same direction and glue in place. Repeat to make a few single and double notes.

INSPIRATIONS

Nailcare novelty tag
Four bottles of different-coloured nail varnish mounted onto a pink card panel make a treat for the eye on this dark purple tag – they look so real, the recipient will be eager to try them out! This would be perfect for presenting a beautycare gift.

Beauty routine
The recess in the front cover of this diary contains a cache of inviting beauty products temptingly revealed through a clear plastic aperture – just the thing for a student following a beauty course or those diehard beauty regime devotees.

Cool phone card
Make your favourite tweeny's day with this state-of-the-art mobile phone card design, with a model that not only plays music but displays a picture of the person who is calling them! The colour scheme could easily be changed for a boy.

Beach life

The seaside is synonymous with relaxation and pleasure, which makes it a sure-fire success as a subject for your quilled creations. And you only need a key motif to cue all those memories of endless sun-drenched, fun-filled days of leisure. You will also be happily entertained playing with coiled paper shapes to create crazy sea creatures, colourful coral and chic beachwear.

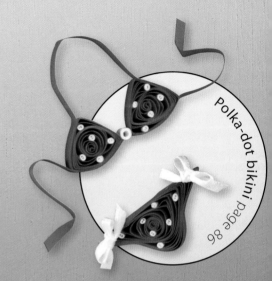

Polka-dot bikini page 86

Delicious ice cream page 87

Staring starfish page 85

Tropical fish and coral page 88

Guppy fish page 89

Characterful crab page 84

Characterful crab

This fun quilled crab is made from bold pink paper, giving it instant appeal to children. Beginning with one large loose coil for the body, his attention-grabbing pincers are created by assembling a series of pinched coils, with the legs formed from smaller shaped coils, so that he really looks ready to scuttle away!

- 3mm (⅛in) wide pink paper
- 2 wiggly eyes, 6mm (¼in) in diameter
- superglue
- Basic Tool Kit (see page 8)

Cut three 45cm (18in) lengths of the pink paper and glue end to end to form a length about 1.35m (53in).

Using your quilling tool, coil the long length of paper into a loose closed coil. Gently squeeze the shape into a crescent with your fingers, trying to avoid pinching the corners, to form the crab's body.

Use a cocktail stick (toothpick) to apply glue to the area on your chosen surface where you want the crab's body to be. Position the crab's body on the glue and hold in place for a few seconds while the glue dries.

For the pincers, make three loose closed coils from 20cm (8in) lengths of the paper for each pincer. Pinch into teardrop shapes (see page 14) and glue together as shown, then glue onto your chosen surface.

For the legs, make eight loose closed coils from 20cm (8in) lengths of the paper, then pinch into leg shapes and glue in place.

Holding a pair of scissors in one hand, pick up a wiggly eye between the points of the blades, and with the other hand, place a dot of superglue on the back of the eye. Position the eye on the edge of the crab's body. Repeat with the other eye.

TIP
You can make the crab from brown paper for a more authentic (and less sunburned!) effect.

Staring starfish

This cute wiggly-eyed sea creature can be made in any bright colour of your choice. For the starfish's legs, strips of paper are inserted into a ribbler (crimper) to make them wavy before being formed into loose closed coils and pinched into shape, which gives them a slightly rippled appearance as if they are floating in the sea.

You will need

- 3mm (1/8in) wide yellow paper
- ribbler (crimper)
- 2 wiggly eyes, 2mm (1/16in) in diameter
- superglue
- Basic Tool Kit (see page 8)

1

Insert a 45cm (18in) length of the paper into the ribbler (crimper) and turn the handle so that the paper is pulled through and ribbled or crimped. Repeat with a further four 45cm (18in) lengths.

2

Make loose closed coils with the five ribbled lengths of paper; be sure not to hold the paper too tightly while coiling.

TIP
If you don't have wiggly eyes, make two closed coils from white strips of paper, adding a dot of black pen to each centre, then attach with PVA (white) glue.

3

Pinch each of the five coils at one end to make long tendril shapes. Make a loose closed coil from a 20cm (8in) length of ribbled paper and glue to your chosen surface. Glue the starfish tendrils around the central coil, holding in place while the glue dries. Glue on the wiggly eyes with superglue (see Step 6 opposite).

INSPIRATIONS

Captivating crab tag
Add a touch of entertainment to a gift package by creating this humorous tag, where this cheeky, 'eye-catching' crab looks like he is about to grab the goodies for himself! The colour scheme can easily be changed to coordinate with the giftwrapping. Alternatively, it could be used to decorate party bags or invitations for a beach or summertime party, or attached to small card shapes to make name badges.

Starfish-struck notebook
Bring novelty value to an ordinary notebook by adding this friendly starfish character to the cover, thereby transforming it into a personalized gift item. It would be perfect for a youngster's holiday journal or scrapbook. Or use it as the focal point for a quirky bon voyage or retirement card.

Polka-dot bikini

The spotted fabric-effect of this classic item of beachwear is convincingly achieved here by inserting small white tight coils into pinched loose closed coil shapes between the inner coils, so that they become integral to them.

You will need
• 3mm (⅛in) wide paper – white, red
• needle tool
• narrow white ribbon
• bow-maker (optional)
• Basic Tool Kit (see page 8)

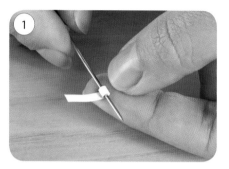

Wrap a 5cm (2in) length of the white paper around a needle tool and glue the end in place.

For the bikini top, make two loose closed coils with 40cm (15¾in) lengths of the red paper and pinch into triangles (see page 14). Repeat with an 80cm (32in) length for the bikini bottom and pinch into a triangular shape. Glue the two smaller triangles to either side of the white coil.

Using the quilling tool, make tight closed coils with 1–1.5cm (⅜– ⅝in) lengths of white paper, turning the tool about three times and gluing the end in place before removing the coil from the tool. Five per bikini triangle are needed.

Pick up the tiny white coils with tweezers and insert into the bikini. If gluing to card, apply glue to the base, but if you are making a freestanding piece, apply glue to the sides of the coils. You may need to use a cocktail stick (toothpick) to push the inner red coils to one side to insert the white coils.

TIP
If you find inserting the white coils too fiddly, you could add very small dots of glitter glue instead.

For a halter-neck strap, glue an 8cm (3⅛in) length of red paper to the outside edges of the triangles. For the back straps, apply glue along the bottom of each triangle and adhere a 4cm (1½in) length of red paper to each. Trim the ends to a point.

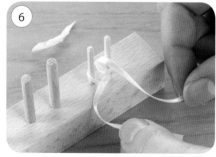

Here, mini white bows were made with narrow ribbon and a bow-maker. Alternatively, you can buy ready-made bows or carefully tie your own. Glue a bow to either side of the bikini bottom.

Delicious ice cream

Weaving with pre-cut strips of paper is another way of adding a further decorative dimension to your quilled designs, and here two different widths and shades of brown paper are woven together to replicate the texture and appearance of a wafer cone, temptingly topped with gently squeezed loose closed coils for scoops of ice cream.

You will need

- 3mm (⅛in) wide brown paper, plus strawberry pink, vanilla cream, pistachio green
- 10mm (⅜in) wide brown paper a shade lighter
- foam block and pins
- double-sided tape
- Basic Tool Kit (see page 8)

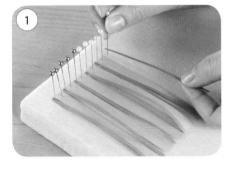

1 Pin strips of brown paper, alternating between the 3mm (⅛in) and 10mm (⅜in) wide, onto a foam block – all the pieces here are 10cm (4in) in length, but it depends on how large you want the ice cream cone to be.

2 Weave a 10mm (⅜in) wide piece of brown paper up and over, then down and under the pinned strips. Pin this at the end to hold it in place. Weave a 3mm (⅛in) wide piece through, starting by going under, then going over. Continue until you have a square of woven paper.

3 Place double-sided tape over the back of all the strips. Leave the backing paper on. Remove the pins and lift the paper from the board.

4 Using the template on page 118, cut out a cone from the woven paper. You can then mount the cone onto your chosen card or other surface using the double-sided tape. You will also need to apply glue to the woven ends that are not stuck with tape. For the ice cream, make three loose closed coils from three 40cm (15¾in) lengths glued together end to end of the pink, vanilla and green paper.

TIP
Alternatively, you could make a woven square and cut out a basket shape to fill with quilled flowers (see Flower Power, pages 38–47).

INSPIRATIONS

Beach babe
A polka-dot bikini will always be in vogue, and here it adorns a bright, sunny card suitable for a teenager, either on the occasion of their summer birthday or as a post-study vacation send-off. The strips of blue checked paper add a snappy complementary trimming to both the tag and card spine.

A cone of note
Transform a workaday notepad by giving it the seaside treatment with this delectable ice cream cone – a gift that's guaranteed to bring an instant lift to any recipient. You can change the ice cream colours to coordinate with the notepad cover and pen.

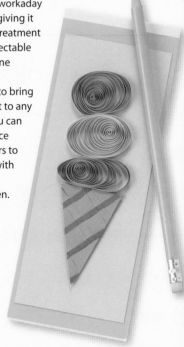

Tropical fish and coral

Create this strikingly marked fish for an exotic underwater design by simply alternating contrasting-coloured loose closed coils, pinched into the appropriate shape. The tail is then ingeniously made to match by hand looping different coloured strips together and forming into a triangle.

You will need

- 3mm (⅛in) wide paper – yellow, blue, black, orange
- 2mm (¹⁄₁₆in) wide pink/orange paper
- wiggly eye, 4mm (⅛in) in diameter
- needle tool
- Basic Tool Kit (see page 8)

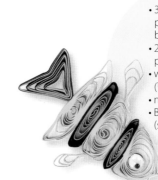

For the head, make a loose closed coil from a 30cm (12in) length of the yellow paper. Pinch the coil at two points on one side, then use a needle tool to pull out a section on the opposite side while pinching it with your fingernail to make a fish mouth shape.

The body is comprised of several loose closed coil shapes: 10cm (4in) of blue glued to 10cm (4in) of black, coiled with the black on the outside; 30cm (12in) of yellow; 15cm (6in) of blue glued to 15cm (6in) of black, coiled with the black on outside; 40cm (15¾in) of yellow; all pinched as shown.

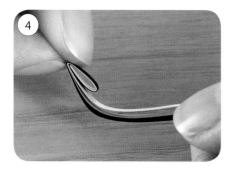

Apply glue to the sides of the pieces and assemble. While the glue is still drying, hold the fish shape and squeeze it together quite firmly.

TIP

Since tropical fish come in all sorts of bright colours, you can use up leftover paper in whatever colours you happen to have.

For the coral, make loose closed coils with 6cm (2⅜in) lengths of the 2mm (¹⁄₁₆in) pink/orange paper and the 3mm (⅛in) wide orange paper, then pinch into bent teardrops (see page 14). Assemble and glue to your chosen surface to resemble coral (see Gone Fishing opposite).

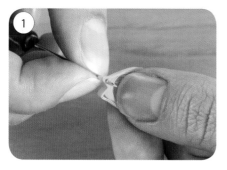

Loop again and glue and then for a third time. Glue the ends and trim the excess – it is easier to work with longer lengths and trim at the end. Flatten the shape by pushing inwards with your finger to make a triangle. Glue to the fish body.

For the tail, glue a length of black, yellow and blue papers together at one end, then form a loop 1cm (⅜in) high with all three papers and glue at the base.

Guppy fish

More than one strip of paper can be coiled at once, and here three different colours are joined end to end to make this eye-catching rainbow-hued fish. And by trimming the beginning of the joined strip to make it narrower, space is cleverly created to insert a wiggly eye so that it sits flush with the fish.

You will need

- 3mm (⅛in) wide paper – dark green, blue, paler green, turquoise
- wiggly eye, 4mm (⅛in) in diameter
- Basic Tool Kit (see page 8)

1

Glue three 40cm (15¾in) lengths of the paper together at one end, one dark green, one blue and one paler green. Cut along the length for 5cm (2in) from the glued end to cut the pieces in half. Trim off one half.

2

Make a loose closed coil, starting at the narrower end, trimming the excess paper at the ends before gluing, as in Step 2, page 33. Pinch the coil into a teardrop shape (see page 14).

3

Place a wiggly eye in the centre of the coil; because this was cut narrower, the eye will be inset slightly.

4

For the fins, make two loose closed coils with 10cm (4in) lengths of the turquoise paper and the tail with a 20cm (8in) length, then pinch into triangular shapes (see page 14). For the mouth, fold a strip of blue paper close to one end, apply glue to the fold and attach to the fish. Leave to dry, then trim the excess paper.

Gone fishing

Here, the tropical fish and coral have been combined to create a convincing underwater scene, complete with tight closed coils for bubbles, glued to a mini door hanger cut from card (template on page 119). You could add a humorous message to the hanger, such as 'I'd rather be scuba diving!'

Fish bowl

For this simple yet highly effective card design, a circle was cut in the front panel of a blue square folded card and acetate mounted behind. The guppy fish and bubbles – again, tight closed coils – were then glued to the acetate to enhance the watery effect, for all those who can't have enough of the sea.

89

Nicely nautical

Sail boats page 95

It can be difficult to find themes that are suitable for males, but these seafaring designs are sure to find favour with many lads and dads, especially when made in traditional nautical colours, which also adds an appealing authenticity. The functional ship's compass will attract the most hardened of sailors, while the jolly flotilla of sailing boats is sure to delight any child.

Boat bunting page 94

Ship's anchor and rope page 93

Quality compass page 92

Stalking seagull

This cheering seabird is a staple of nautical life, and can be successfully constructed from a combination of three different pinched coils. To achieve the subtle colouring on the wings and body, grey ink from an inkpad is rubbed onto white coils with a cotton bud, so that you can control where the colour is applied and how much.

You will need

- 3mm (⅛in) wide paper – white, black, yellow, orange
- grey inkpad
- cotton bud
- Basic Tool Kit (see page 8)

For the body, make a loose closed coil from a 40cm (15¾in) length of the white paper and pinch into a teardrop (see page 14). Repeat for the wing but with a 30cm (12in) length of paper. Press a cotton bud into the inkpad to pick up some grey ink. Rub the cotton bud onto the edge of the body to colour the paper.

TIP

The seagull need not have legs; it could be depicted resting on an anchor – see page 93.

For the head, glue a 1cm (⅜in) length of the black paper to a 25cm (10in) length of white paper. Start coiling tightly from the black paper, and when the white is reached, add a dot of glue, then continue coiling to make a loose closed coil. Pinch very slightly into a head shape. Apply ink as in Step 1. For the beak, fold a length of yellow paper into a 'W' shape and glue inside the fold. Glue to the head.

For the legs and feet, make three mini concertina folds in the centre of a 4cm (1½in) length of the orange paper, each about 2mm (⅟₁₆in) wide.

Apply glue inside each fold and along the length and press together. Repeat to make the second leg and foot. Assemble and glue the bird together, with the wing on top of the body.

INSPIRATIONS

Tagged seagull

A single seagull is glued to a disc of deep blue card punched and threaded with matching blue cord to make a cute tag – perhaps for a going-away gift for someone departing on a birthday or anniversary cruise.

Noteworthy seabird

Two seagulls have been used here to decorate the cover of a small spiral-bound notebook – the ideal gift for a budding birdwatcher. Note how you can vary the stance of the bird by the way in which the head and legs are positioned, for added animation and visual interest.

91

Quality compass

Every sailor or sea fisherman needs a good compass and here pinched quilled coils applied to concentric circles of card in two layers point the way. This design illustrates yet another use for the versatile pinched teardrop shape.

You will need

• blue card
• 3mm (⅛in) wide black paper
• 2mm (¹⁄₁₆in) wide red paper
• graph paper
• red brad
• circular protractor or compass
• quilling board (optional)
• adhesive foam pads
• Basic Tool Kit (see page 8)

Draw around the circular protractor onto graph paper or use a compass to draw a 10cm (4in) diameter circle. Divide the circle into quarters and each quarter into four equal segments. Then add three inner circles, 7.5cm (3in), 5cm (2in) and 2.5cm (1in) in diameter. Cut three circles from blue card the same diameter as these three circles.

Place the largest card circle on the drawn circle and draw in the dissecting lines, leaving out the North–South (vertical) and East–West (horizontal) axes. Use faint pencil marks – here, darker pencil lines were used in order to show up in the photo. Place the smaller circle in position and draw in the remaining axes.

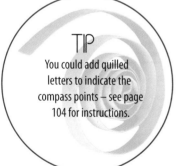

Make 24 loose closed coils with 20cm (8in) lengths of the black paper and pinch into teardrops (see page 14) – you may want to use a quilling board to ensure that they are all the same size. Glue to the largest circle along the marked lines, points outwards and aligned with the edge.

Make four teardrops in the same way with 40cm (15¾in) lengths of the black paper. Glue along the marked lines on the smaller circle, points outwards but overlapping the edge. Insert a brad into the centre of the smallest circle, then mount onto the larger circle with adhesive foam pads.

TIP
You could add quilled letters to indicate the compass points – see page 104 for instructions.

Ship's anchor and rope

This sturdy-looking anchor is constructed from a combination of simple loose closed coil components, pinched and bent into shape, apart from the top ring, which is formed around a wooden spoon handle or dowel. The challenge here is to match both sides of the anchor as closely as possible.

You will need

• 3mm (⅛in) wide paper – grey, white
• wooden spoon or dowel, 7mm (¼in) in diameter
• Basic Tool Kit (see page 8)

Wrap a 30cm (12in) length of the grey paper around the handle of the wooden spoon or dowel, glue the end in place and remove. Make two loose closed coils from 40cm (15¾in) lengths, pinch each into two corners at one end and press flat at the other. Make two loose closed coils with 30cm (12in) lengths, then pinch into arrow shapes as shown, and two with 20cm (8in) lengths, then squeeze flat for the cross pieces.

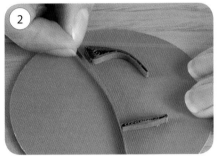

Glue one of the long pinched coils for the bottom of the anchor to your chosen surface, bending the flat end upwards and holding in place while the glue dries. Glue one of the cross pieces in place. For the central piece of the anchor, glue two 6.5cm (2½in) lengths of the grey paper together lengthways, then curve slightly and glue at right angles to the bottom and cross pieces.

Glue on the second bottom and cross pieces on the other side of the anchor, as in Step 2. Add the round coil to the top.

For the rope, make several loose closed coils with 8cm (3⅛in) lengths of the white paper. Pinch each into an 'S' shape, then glue together as shown for a linked effect.

TIP
The rope could be made with brown or blue paper instead, or for a racing sailor, use bright colours such as green or red.

INSPIRATIONS

Directional design
The quilled compass simply mounted onto a deep blue square folded card makes a memorable design for a sailor, orienteer, walker or hiker. Alternatively, attach it to the cover of a photo or scrapbook album for capturing those great adventures over land or sea.

Artistically anchored
Transform a plain notebook into a sea captain's logbook with the quilled anchor motif. Simply mount onto a red card circle and attach the rope to the top of the anchor, letting it trail off onto the notebook cover. The same design could be used for a striking bon voyage card.

Boat bunting

These bright and breezy ship's flags, in traditional nautical colours, are quick and easy to make by sticking together pinched coil rectangles and triangles in different combinations, except for a clever trick used for the yellow flag, where the centre of a pinched square is cut out to make way for a black coil.

You will need

• 3mm (⅛in) wide paper – yellow, black, white, bright blue, red
• quilling board
• Basic Tool Kit (see page 8)

For the yellow flag, make a loose closed coil with a 40cm (15¾in) length of the yellow paper and pinch into a square (see page 14). Using the points of a small pair of scissors, cut out the centre of the coil and discard. Make a loose closed coil from an 8cm (3⅛in) length of the black paper. Insert into the centre of the yellow square.

For the blue and white flag, make a loose closed coil from a 40cm (15¾in) length of the white paper and pinch into a rectangle (see page 15). Make two loose closed coils from 20cm (8in) lengths of the blue paper and pinch into right-angled triangles (see page 14). Try to make the paper join on the side that will be glued to the white rectangle. Glue the triangles to the white rectangle.

For the red and yellow flag, make a coil with a 40cm (15¾in) length of the red and yellow papers. Apply glue to the end of each, insert into the 1.6mm (1/16in) diameter circle template of a quilling board and release, to make a uniform size. Pinch the loose closed coils into right-angled triangles, with the paper join on the longest side, and glue together.

TIP
Restrict the colours to traditionally nautical ones for an authentic look.

For the red and blue flag, make a red and blue loose closed coil with 40cm (15¾in) lengths using a quilling board, as in Step 3. Pinch into rectangles, with the paper join on the longest side, and glue together.

For the red, white and blue flag, glue a 10cm (4in) length of the red paper to a 20cm (8in) length of the white, then glue the white to a 30cm (12in) length of the blue. Start coiling from the red paper and make a loose closed coil, then pinch into a square.

For the red flag, make a loose closed coil from a 60cm (23¾in) length of the red paper and pinch two corners on one side, then pinch into two triangular shapes on the other.

Sail boats

These simple, stylized boats are especially designed to appeal to children, and here the sails can be any mixture of bright colours that will attract and maintain their attention.

You will need
• 3mm (⅛in) wide paper – red, blue, pale blue, dark blue, brown
• 2mm (¹⁄₁₆in) blue paper
• Basic Tool Kit (see page 8)

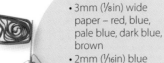

For the three boats, the large and small sails for each (left to right) consist of loose closed coils made with a 30cm (12in) length of red, a 20cm (8in) length of 3mm (⅛in) blue, a 40cm (15¾in) length of pale blue, a 40cm (15¾in) length of dark blue, a 30cm (12in) length of blue and a 20cm (8in) length of red, each pinched into triangles (see page 14).

For the boat hulls, make loose closed coils with a 40cm (15¾in) length of the 3mm (⅛in) dark blue paper and 30cm (12in) lengths of the pale blue and blue 3mm (⅛in) papers. Pinch into shape and glue onto your chosen surface, with the larger hull in the centre.

Glue the three larger triangles above each hull. For the masts, glue vertical lengths of the brown paper trimmed to measure 2.5cm (1in) for the smaller boats and 3.5cm (1⅜in) for the larger one. For the red flag, make a loose closed coil with a 20cm (8in) length of the red paper, pinch into shape and glue at the top of the large boat's mast.

For the waves, cut 2–3cm (¾–1⅛in) lengths of the 2mm (¹⁄₁₆in) blue paper and coil at one end without gluing. Glue beneath the boats.

Flying colours

For this uplifting card design, the six flying flags are glued to a length of cord threaded through a double set of holes that has been punched either side of the folded card and fixed with eyelets. Short lengths of the rope tied into a sailing knot add an extra nautical note. This would be ideal for sending a message of congratulations on passing an important exam or test.

Sailing team tag

The three jolly quilled boats are seen bobbing along on a pale blue card panel mounted onto a darker blue rectangular tag threaded and tied with white sheer ribbon – a lovely design for a baby or young child's gift. It would make an equally effective greetings card for an adult sailing enthusiast.

Cooking capers

Liven up your kitchen – and those of your friends and family – with some cunningly quilled culinary items. Ceramic storage jars, for instance, can be transformed by the addition of delicate herb sprigs, bright red chillies and plump olives, or a metal tin jazzed up with coffee beans. Alternatively, use to create unique greetings cards for aspiring chefs.

Red hot chilli pepper page 98

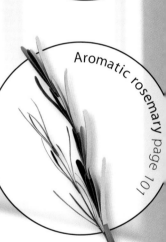

Aromatic rosemary page 101

Flowering thyme

Olive sprig page 99

Real coffee

These coffee beans are proof that just about anything can be made with quilling! They are created with miraculous ease by gluing together two crescent-shaped pinched coils. Any shade of brown paper can be used and the shapes are best when not uniform, so several can be made in a short space of time.

You will need
• 3mm (⅛in) wide paper – brown, cream
• Basic Tool Kit (see page 8)

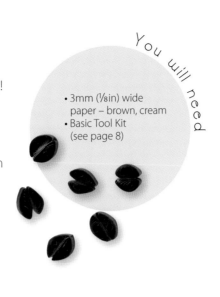

1 Make loose closed coils with 10cm (4in) lengths of the brown paper. You will need two per coffee bean, so decide how many you need.

2 Pinch each coil into a crescent shape (see page 14), making sure that the join is at the top, pressing your fingernails inwards on either side.

3 Take two crescent shapes and place glue along the flat edge of one. Press the flat side of the other shape to the glue and hold in place for a few seconds while the glue dries.

4 To make steam, cut 5cm (2in) lengths of the cream paper and make an open coil in the end of each one. Remove the tool and use your fingers to open the coil a little further. Use a fingernail to curl the other end of the paper.

TIP
Real coffee beans are many shades of brown, so add a few beans made in different brown papers.

INSPIRATIONS

Café sensation

A decorative border of quilled coffee beans is combined here with a coffee mug cut from brown card (template on page 119) and rising coils of steam, mounted onto a pink folded card. A side panel of script-printed paper adds to the sophisticated, café society-style feel of the design. This would be ideal for a 'come round for coffee' or 'let's meet up for a chat' invitation, either for a friend or as a welcome to a newcomer to quilling.

Coffee coaster

This transparent plastic coaster with a built-in recess features a coffee mug (template on page 119) cut from a piece of brown patterned paper with steam curls rising from it, framed by a scattering of coffee beans. This is ideal for resting your reviving beverage on when you are busy quilling!

Red hot chilli pepper

This amazingly realistic red chilli is created from a quilled cone shape, as for the carrots and tool handles in the Gardening gems chapter (see pages 24, 26 and 29), but then deliberately misshapen to create its characteristic twisted, slightly crumpled appearance – you can be quite rough with the cone after the glue inside has dried. The final coating of glue gives it an authentic shiny skin.

You will need

• 3mm (⅛in) wide paper – red, green
• sheet of acetate
• Basic Tool Kit (see page 8)

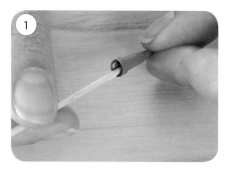

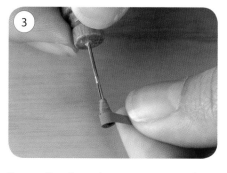

Insert one end of a 20cm (8in) length of the red paper into your quilling tool. Coil tightly for three turns, then continue to turn the tool but angle the paper away from the tool and make sure that the paper overlaps enough to create an elongated cone shape (see Step 3, page 24). Using a cocktail stick (toothpick), apply glue all the way down inside the cone – it is important to leave it to dry thoroughly.

Glue a 4cm (1½in) length of the green paper to a 5cm (2in) length of the red paper end to end.

Start coiling from the green paper as if you are making a cone, then when the red paper is reached, stop angling the paper to produce a flat coil. Glue the end in place.

TIP
You can vary the lengths of the papers used to make chillies of different sizes, or use green paper to make green chillies.

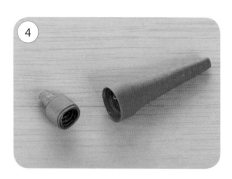

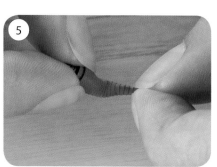

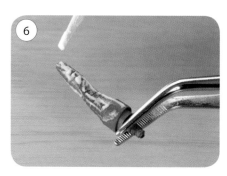

Insert into the red elongated cone. Make several cones and tops and then assemble, as they will all be fractionally different sizes, so if one doesn't fit, you can try another.

Pinch, press and squeeze the cone to make it look chilli-like, but avoid pulling it, otherwise the cone will unravel, despite being glued inside.

Hold the end with tweezers and apply a good coat of PVA (white) glue all over the chilli. To avoid it sticking, place on acetate to dry. When dry, remove from the acetate and glue to your chosen surface or object.

Olive sprig

Real olives come in differing hues of green and black, and also vary in size, so let nature be your guide in making these olive sprigs convincing. The fruits are formed from tightly coiled long lengths of paper, with the inner edge gently pushed out to create a domed shape.

You will need
- 3mm (⅛in) wide paper – olive green and/or black, sea green
- Basic Tool Kit (see page 8)

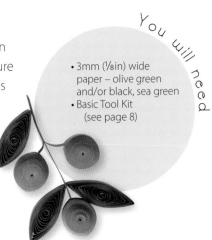

Glue three 40cm (15¾in) lengths of the olive green paper together end to end. For black olives, glue two 40cm (15¾in) lengths of the black paper together end to end. Use to make tight closed coils, holding your fingertip over the end to keep the coil flat.

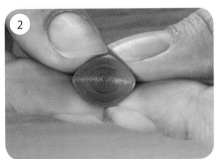

Using the nails of both thumbs, push up the inner edge of the coil (see Step 1, page 25); try to avoid pushing up the centre, as this makes the shape too high. Spread glue all over the inside and leave to dry, then pinch the shape into an oval.

For the stalk, cut an 8cm (3⅛in) length of the sea green paper and place on scrap paper. Cut 5cm (2in) lengths of the paper and spread with glue, stopping 1cm (⅜in) from the end. Press the glued lengths onto the longer length. These lengths can vary depending on how long you want the olive sprig.

For the leaves, make loose closed coils from 40cm (15¾in) of the sea green paper. Pinch both at opposing points to make leaf shapes, ensuring that the join is at one end. Apply glue to the ends and attach to the stalk. Leaves for the black olives are made from 20cm (8in) lengths of the same green paper.

INSPIRATIONS

Turn up the heat

For this eye-catching gift item, a small square of bright green card was placed inside a transparent plastic key ring with a recess, then three red chillies glued vertically in alternating directions to the card and the lid replaced. The chillies were slightly squashed in the process, but this only adds to the effect. This design would also make a great gift tag for a kitchen-related present.

Italian job

Delight even the most discerning food connoisseur with a bottle of top-quality extra virgin olive oil and fashion your own special label, decorated with quilled sprigs of both black and green olives. Alternatively, a sprig or two of olives could be mounted onto a rectangular piece of card, then punched and threaded with raffia and tied around the bottle neck.

Flowering thyme

The petite flowers of this favourite culinary herb are re-created in quilling using the hand-looping method, in a similar way to the leaves on page 46, but in this case on a tiny scale. If you find this technique too fiddly, you can use the husking technique instead (see page 16), inserting pins into a board and wrapping the papers around them, to make slightly larger flowers.

You will need

- 3mm (⅛in) wide paper – pink, dark green, brown
- Basic Tool Kit (see page 8)

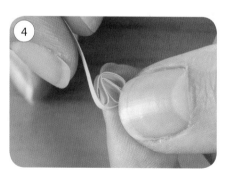

1 For the flowers, bend rather than fold over 5mm (³⁄₁₆in) at one end of a 15cm (6in) length of the pink paper.

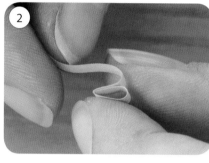

2 Take the paper strip round and up the other side of the end of the paper to form a loop.

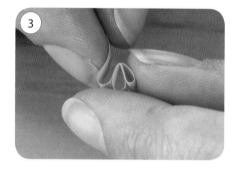

3 Take the paper back round the other side to make a loop on the other side of the first loop.

TIP

As the thyme sprig is very small, you may wish to use a magnifier to make it (see page 10).

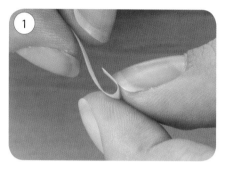

5 For the herb leaves, make small loose closed coils with 4cm (1½in) lengths of the dark green paper. For the stem, glue two 10cm (4in) lengths of the brown paper together lengthways. Glue a leaf to the end of the stem.

6 Glue a flower to the leaf and then glue a leaf the other side, then two more leaves either side. Use both hands to hold in place while the glue dries. Glue another flower further down the stem with two leaves. Continue in the same way to complete the sprig.

4 Take the paper right the way round the three loops to encapsulate them and then trim the end and glue in place. Each flower uses a length of paper 5–6cm (2–2⅜in), but it is easier to use a longer piece and trim the end. Make several flowers.

Aromatic rosemary

Quilling papers can be used in a variety of ways, not just for coiling. The needle-like leaves of this highly scented herb are surprisingly easy to replicate by gluing a grey and green strip of paper together lengthways and trimming to round at one end.

You will need
- 3mm (⅛in) wide paper – green, grey, brown
- Basic Tool Kit (see page 8)

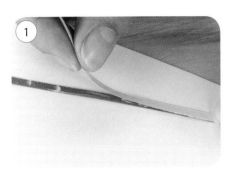

1 For the leaves, place a 10cm (4in) length of the green paper on scrap paper. Apply glue along the entire length. Top with a 10cm (4in) length of the grey paper.

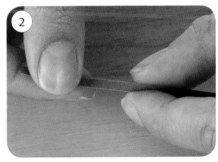

2 Pick up the glued-together papers and run your fingertips down either side to ensure that the papers are glued down thoroughly and the edges are even.

3 Cut 3cm (1⅛in) and 2cm (¾in) lengths from the glued-together papers. Round one end of each piece with scissors.

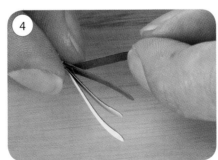

4 For the stem, cut a 10cm (4in) length of the brown paper. Glue the leaves to the stem in groups of four (two leaves either side), with the smaller leaves on the inside and the grey side facing outwards.

TIP
When gluing the lengths of paper together, your hands will become sticky, so wash them regularly.

INSPIRATIONS

Thyme to celebrate
A delicate sprig of flowering thyme is used here to make a charming greetings card suitable for all kinds of purposes – for a get well or thank you message or to mark the occasion of Mother's Day or a birthday. It would also make a lovely motif for the cover of a cook's diary or recipe cuttings folder.

Herbal helper
Two sprigs of rosemary tied with pretty satin ribbon and glued to a wooden plant label make a welcome gift for someone who loves to grow their own culinary herbs – it could be packaged up with a seed tray and herb seeds. Alternatively, you could glue a magnet to the underside to make a foodie fridge magnet.

Party time

Take the opportunity to introduce a new generation to the wonderful craft of quilling with party bags, place cards and gift tags decorated with quilled designs – that way, it's sure to endure for the next 500 years! Here are easily made, brightly coloured balloons and 3-D tactile candles, together with letters and numbers to create personalized items of party ware.

Letters and numbers page 104

Flaming candles page 105

Floating balloon

Balloons are a perennial party favourite and are quick to quill, being formed from two loose closed coils, one large and slightly pinched for the main shape and the other small and pinched into a triangle for the base. The former looks most effective when the inner coils are positioned centrally, so are best made in a quilling board and manipulated accordingly.

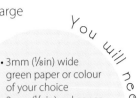

You will need

- 3mm (⅛in) wide green paper or colour of your choice
- 2mm (¹⁄₁₆in) red paper or contrasting colour of your choice
- quilling board
- Basic Tool Kit (see page 8)

1

Make a coil with a 40cm (15¾in) length of the 3mm (⅛in) wide paper. Apply glue to the end, then insert the coil into the 2cm (¾in) diameter template in the quilling board. Let the coil release to fit the circle. Use a pin to bring the coil centre to the edge where the paper join is, press the pin into the board and apply a dot of glue to hold in place (see Steps 2–3, page 79). Remove the pin and shape and pinch the coil slightly to make a balloon shape.

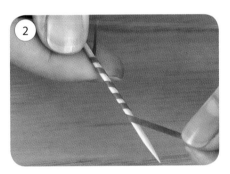

2

Wrap a 10cm (4in) length of the 2mm (¹⁄₁₆in) wide paper around a clean cocktail stick (toothpick). Hold one end in place with one hand and continue wrapping it around with the other hand. Then slide the stick out.

3

Make a loose closed coil with a 15cm (6in) length of the 3mm (⅛in) paper and pinch into a triangle (see page 14). Glue the spiral to the base of the balloon shape and then glue on the triangle, sandwiching the spiral between the other two shapes.

TIP
You could make a big balloon from a long length of paper formed from several lengths glued end to end and add peel-off sticker numbers for a milestone birthday, such as 40 or 21.

INSPIRATIONS

Spiral-bound balloons
Give a birthday celebration a memorable send-off with this balloon bonanza, three tied down and another floating free. The surrounding card is decorated with open coils made with 5cm (2in) and 10cm (4in) lengths of 2mm (¹⁄₁₆in) wide papers in a variety of colours for added pizzazz.

Birthday streamers
A quick tag has been made here with two floating balloons tied with spiral streamers in a limited colour scheme. Three ribbon ties in coordinating colours add to the breezy effect. The design could be adapted to make party invitations.

Letters and numbers

Capital letters look particularly decorative in quilling and are deceptively easy to make. The following instructions show you how to make A, B and C, but by applying the same principles of folding, coiling and gluing the components together, the whole alphabet can be quilled (see page 92 for further examples). Stylish numbers are just as simple to create in the same way.

You will need
• 3mm (⅛in) wide paper in the colour of your choice
• Basic Tool Kit (see page 8)

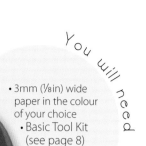

For the letter A, fold a 15cm (6in) length in half and coil both ends. Make an 'S' scroll (see Step 3, page 52) with a 5cm (2in) length of the same paper and then position this in the centre for the cross bar.

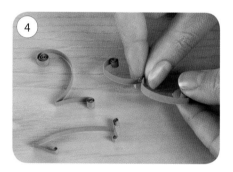

For the letter B, coil either end of a 5cm (2in) length towards each other. Fold a 10cm (4in) length in half and apply a dot of glue to the fold. Coil the ends outwards, then glue to the first length.

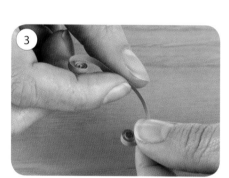

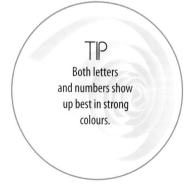

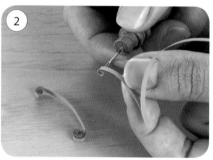

Numbers 1–9 are made in the same way as the letters, as shown. These are the lengths required for each; the measurements can be made larger or smaller so long as the proportions remain the same. Number 1: 7cm (2¾in) and 3cm (1⅛in). Number 2: 15cm (6in). Number 3: 15cm (6in).

For the letter C, coil either end of a 15cm (6in) length, but use your fingernail to curl the centre portion.

Number 4: two 6cm (2⅜in) and one 9cm (3½in) – fold one of the shorter lengths in half, then fold down each end to create a 'V' shape with horizontal wings; coil one end of the longer length, then glue the closed 'V' over the uncoiled end; coil both ends of the remaining length and glue one end to the left-hand wing to form the short upright. Number 5: 15cm (6in). Number 6: 18cm (7in).

Number 7: 12cm (4¾in). Number 8: 20cm (8in). Number 9: 15cm (6in).

TIP
Both letters and numbers show up best in strong colours.

Flaming candles

Freestanding 3-D quilled candles are sure to attract attention and are simply formed from loose closed coils pinched into upright oblongs. Glue is applied to the reverse side of the shapes and then they are left to dry on easily removable acetate, which makes them rigid and able to hold the weight of the coiled flame.

You will need
• 3mm (⅛in) wide papers in bright colours of your choice, plus red, orange, yellow
• 2mm (¹⁄₁₆in) wide white paper
• sheet of acetate
• card
• gold pen
• Basic Tool Kit (see page 8)

1

Make a loose closed coil with a 40cm (15¾in) length of a 3mm (⅛in) wide paper, then pinch into a long rectangular shape (see page 15). Apply glue to one side, then place on the sheet of acetate. Hold in position for a few seconds while the glue dries. Make as many candles as you need in different colours, lining them up on the acetate.

2

Leave the candles for at least an hour to ensure that all the glue is thoroughly dry. Then remove the acetate from the candles by bending it away from them – don't try to pull the candles off.

TIP
You don't have to use acetate, but you need to use a flexible type of plastic.

3

For a flame, glue a 5cm (2in) length of the red paper to 5cm (2in) of the orange and then to 10cm (4in) of the yellow end to end and make a loose closed coil, starting from the red end. Pinch the coil into a flame shape. Glue to a candle. Repeat for the remaining candles.

4

Glue the candle to your chosen card or other surface, in this case by just adding a small amount of glue to the lower part (see Candle Cupcake right) – the candles are strong enough to be freestanding.

INSPIRATIONS

Best badges
Decorative quilled numbers mounted onto simple badges can be used to celebrate a special date, birthday or anniversary. They can be attached to a card or presented to party guests on the day to wear.

Candle cupcake
A single candle stands upright from a folded place card to make a dynamic design for a party table. The card cake shape (template on page 116) is mounted onto the card with an adhesive foam pad to create enough depth for the decorative topping of open coils made from 2mm (¹⁄₁₆in) wide white paper.

105

Christmas crackers

The festive season is the ideal time to get quilling and offers the perfect excuse to indulge in luxurious metallic-edged papers for that extra glamour and sparkle. But Christmas quilled decorations need not be glitzy. See, for example, the ornate snowflake made entirely from coiled white paper or the naturalistic beauty of the holly, ivy and mistletoe.

Festive foliage page 112

Curly Christmas tree page 110

Bauble embellishment page 113

Stripy stocking page 111

3-D snowflake page 108

Sparkling snowflake page 106

3-D snowflake

Pure white shows quilling to its best effect because the focus is on the shapes and the light flowing through the pinched coils, and this elaborately patterned snowflake demonstrates this principle perfectly. As it is a complex design, a foam block and pins are used to help hold the coils and pinched shapes in place. The wider paper makes the decoration more hard-wearing.

You will need

- 5mm (³/₁₆in) wide white paper
- graph paper
- parchment (translucent) paper
- blue or clear cotton
- foam block and pins
- Basic Tool Kit (see page 8)

1 Using a pencil and ruler, mark out on graph paper the eight evenly spaced axes for the snowflake. Place parchment paper over the top and pin both to a foam block.

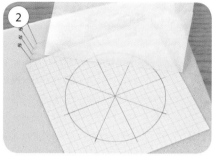

2 Make a loose closed coil with a 10cm (4in) length of the white paper. Position on the centre of the circle and pin in place. Do not apply any glue to the underside.

3 Make four loose closed coils with 20cm (8in) lengths of the white paper and pinch into teardrops (see page 14). Glue the rounded ends inwards around the central circle, aligning with the cross axes. Use pins to hold in place while the glue dries.

TIP

The parchment paper not only stops the pencil from spoiling the quilling paper, but it can be used to catch any glue, thereby protecting your template.

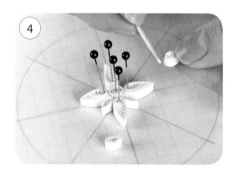

4 Make another four teardrops with 10cm (4in) lengths of the white paper. Glue in between the previous teardrops, aligning with the other four axes.

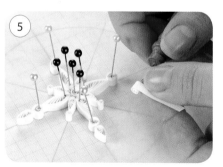

5 The next shape on the long axes is a loose closed coil made with a 10cm (4in) length of paper, then a teardrop made with a 10cm (4in) length. For the other axes, make a tight closed coil with a 5cm (2in) length and a teardrop with a 10cm (4in) length. Pin all the shapes in place.

6 Leave for about an hour to let the glue dry thoroughly. Remove the pins and then lift the snowflake from the parchment paper. Thread a length of cotton through a top coil and tie in a knot for hanging.

Sparkling snowflake

In this strikingly sophisticated design, open coils are used to encapsulate pinched loose closed coils – a technique known as 'nesting' – to produce a delicate, tracery effect that is still contemporary in style. Other unusual designs can be built up using this approach.

- 3mm (⅛in) wide silver-edged blue paper
- Basic Tool Kit (see page 8)

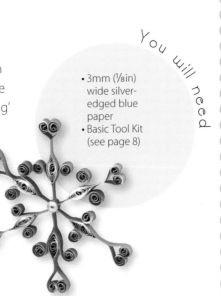

Quality crystal
The intricate white snowflake makes a bold statement set against a seasonal red card square threaded with green ribbon for a special gift tag. Alternatively, it is dramatic enough to take pride of place at the top of the tree. Be sure to keep well away from naked flames for safety.

1

Make a loose closed coil with a 10cm (4in) length of the paper. Pinch at two opposing points. Fold a 10cm (4in) length of the paper in half, then apply glue for 1.3cm (½in) on one side of the fold. Insert the pinched coil into the fold, making sure that the metallic edges are facing the same way. Press the paper to the coil to wrap it.

2

Coil each end of the paper towards each other and remove the tool without gluing.

TIP
Snowflakes don't have to be blue or white – be ultra modern and make them pink, red or silver, or to coordinate with your festive theme.

3

Fold another 10cm (4in) length of the paper in half, apply glue as in Step 1 and press together. Then apply glue as before, insert the teardrop coil and press the paper to the coil. Coil the ends of the paper outwards.

4

Repeat to make six snowflake pieces in all. Glue around a central tight closed coil made with a 10cm (4in) length of paper.

Snowflake centrepiece
This icy blue snowflake is mounted onto a blue card circle and suspended in a circular aperture cut in the folded card front so that it will turn slightly and the silver edging will shimmer in the light. The snowflake circle could be preserved for the following year and hung on the Christmas tree.

Curly Christmas tree

The branches of this elegant festive tree are created by folding paper strips in half, gluing to a central stem by the fold and making open coils in the free ends. It is then hung with a variety of delightful mini decorations, including coiled and pinched hearts, star and gift box, the latter decorated with a bow formed from two tiny teardrops.

You will need

• 3mm (⅛in) wide paper – green edged with metallic green, ivory/gold, red, pink, blue/silver, pale blue, orange, pink/copper
• Basic Tool Kit (see page 8)

For the stem, fold a 40cm (15¾in) length of the green paper in half. Place on scrap paper. Glue 10cm (4in) along from the fold. Fold the other half of the paper over and press together, leaving the two ends free.

For the side branches, cut 22cm (9in), 26cm (10¼in), 30cm (12in) and 34cm (13½in) lengths of the same paper. Fold each in half and glue at the fold to the central stem, leaving the ends free.

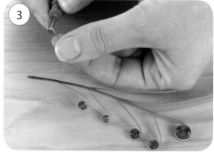

Coil the ends of the branches away from the central stem without gluing the coils.

Make a loose closed coil with a 40cm (15¾in) length of the ivory/gold paper. Pinch into a star (see page 15). Repeat with a 20cm (8in) length of the red paper, but pinch into a heart (see page 15). Make a tiny loop from pink paper. For the baubles, make loose closed coils with 10cm (4in) and 8cm (3⅛in) lengths of the blue/silver and pale blue paper. Pinch the latter into a rectangle (see page 15), glue to the former and add a loop. Repeat with 15cm (6in) and 10cm (4in) lengths of leftover papers.

For the gift box, make a loose closed coil with a 40cm (15¾in) length of the orange paper and pinch into a square (see page 14). Wrap two lengths of the pink/copper paper crossways around the present and glue to the underside.

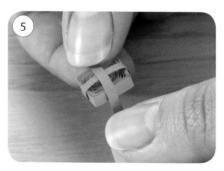

For the bow, make two loose closed coils with 10cm (4in) lengths of the pink/copper paper and pinch into teardrops (see page 14). Glue together at the points. Curl either end of a 5cm (2in) length of the same paper inwards. Glue to the top of the present and attach the bow.

Stripy stocking

This traditional seasonal motif demonstrates another creative way to use pre-cut strips of paper designed for quilling. The stripy patterned 'fabric' is made by gluing wide and thin strips of pink and cream paper to paler pink card. The plain stocking top is embellished with loose closed coils in coordinating colours.

You will need

- 10mm (³⁄₈in) wide pink paper
- 3mm (¹⁄₈in) wide ivory/cream paper
- 2mm (¹⁄₁₆in) wide paper – pink, green, dark pink
- card – pink, 20 x 5cm (8 x 6in), red
- Basic Tool Kit (see page 8)

1 Spread glue all the way along a length of the 10mm (³⁄₈in) wide pink paper, then press onto the pink card. Continue to add lengths at evenly spaced intervals in the same way across the card.

2 Glue lengths of the 3mm (¹⁄₈in) wide ivory/cream paper on top of the existing strips, positioning them centrally.

3 Using the template on page 119, cut out a stocking from the stripy card, placing the template at an angle to the strips. If you want to create a freestanding stocking, position the template so that you can cut a second stocking from the card.

4 Using the template on page 119, cut out a stocking top from red card, or two if freestanding, and glue to the stocking. Make loose closed coils with 10cm (4in) lengths of the 2mm (¹⁄₁₆in) wide pink, green and dark pink paper, then glue to the points of the stocking top and along the top edge. Form a length of paper into a loop and attach to the stocking top at the back. If freestanding, decorate both sides in the same way, then glue together around the edges, sandwiching the loop in between.

TIP
By making your own striped card, you can make it coordinate perfectly with your paper coils.

Trendy tree card
Offering a modern twist on the traditional, this minimalist Christmas tree makes a stylish motif for a deluxe festive card. But why stop there? You could change the colour of the tree to white, pink or even black set against a suitably contrasting background for a design with attitude.

Great expectations
For a characterful Christmas card design, simply mount the stripy stocking onto a pale-coloured card panel for maximum contrast and in turn onto a coordinating pink folded card. Glue a mini clothes peg to the loop so that the stocking really looks like it is hanging up, waiting to be filled with festive treats.

Festive foliage

Greenery plays a leading role in decorations for the festive season, and is equally appealing in quilled form. So here's how to re-create the classic trio – holly, ivy and mistletoe – from pinched loose closed coils. The pinching technique for the first two requires a little practise to perfect and care should be taken in selecting the appropriate shades of green paper.

You will need

• 3mm (⅛in) wide paper – dark green, red edged with metallic red, olive green, green, white
• Basic Tool Kit (see page 8)

For the holly, make a loose closed coil from a 20cm (8in) length of the dark green paper, then pinch into an eye shape (see page 14).

Hold the shape in the centre with the index and thumbnail of one hand and pinch the end of the shape while simultaneously pushing inwards.

Turn the shape around and repeat with the other end, pinching and pushing inwards, then let the shape go and gently push both ends together to achieve a holly shape. For the berries, make tight closed coils with 2–3cm (¾–1⅛in) lengths of the red paper.

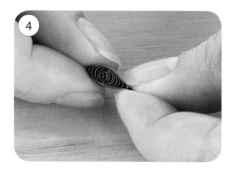

For ivy, make a loose closed coil with a 20cm (8in) length of the olive green paper. Pinch into a teardrop shape with the centre at one end (see page 15). Pinch the other end tight with your fingernails.

While still holding in this position, push the shape over your fingernail. Release and give the shape a gentle push to achieve the ivy shape. Make smaller ivy leaves with 15cm (6in) and 10cm (4in) lengths.

For mistletoe, make two loose closed coils with 40cm (15¾in) lengths of the green paper. Pinch into eye shapes with the centre towards one end. For the berries, make two tight closed coils with 10cm (4in) lengths of the white paper. Assemble with a small 2cm (¾in) length of green paper for the stem.

Bauble embellishment

The 'nesting' technique, featured in the snowflake on page 109, is again used here to create this ornate, Eastern-inspired decoration for a festive bauble. This time, however, the coils that are encased are all open coils.

You will need

- 2mm (¹⁄₁₆in) wide paper – shades of purple and mauve
- Basic Tool Kit (see page 8)

1 Fold two 10cm (4in) lengths of paper in two different shades of purple in half, then glue together only at the very fold.

2 Coil each length down to the fold so the coils are staggered and the colours alternate.

3 Coil the alternating coloured lengths in varying directions and leave open.

4 Fold a 10cm (4in) length of dark purple paper in half, then glue the coiled piece to the fold. Glue the ends of the dark purple paper together, encapsulating the coils, then trim the excess.

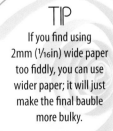

TIP
If you find using 2mm (¹⁄₁₆in) wide paper too fiddly, you can use wider paper; it will just make the final bauble more bulky.

INSPIRATIONS

The holly and the ivy
This luxury card offers a feast of festive foliage for those who relish a new take on traditional seasonal decorations. A wreath is created from holly attached in pairs with red berries around a green card circle topped with a gold bow, while the garland consists of ivy leaves glued either side of a length of the olive green paper.

Under the mistletoe
Make your gift stand out from the crowd with this quick and easy tag featuring a sprig of mistletoe mounted onto layered card circles in classic Christmas green and red. The outside circle could be cut with fancy-edged scissors and the decoration hung from the tree.

Hanging treasure
For this opulent card design, the bauble shapes were die-cut from coloured card, then a second set die-cut from silver card and the tops trimmed off. These tops were glued to the quilling-embellished baubles and threaded with gold ribbon.

Decorated gift boxes and bags

While gift boxes and bags are easy to make, you may want to save the time involved and buy ready-made ones so that you can concentrate your efforts on making quilled embellishments for them instead. Boxes are available in a variety of shapes and sizes, as are gift bags, which often come with a printed pattern that can be incorporated into your quilling design. If you have made a quilled card, you can then decorate a gift box or bag and tag to tie in with the theme.

Colour karma

This CD box has been tied with orange ribbon around two corners and tied in a bow. A large oriental-style quilled flower (see page 72) was glued to the centre, with six smaller flowers either side (see page 73) – all unconnected by stems to create a 'Zen' feel. This would make an ideal package for a Mother's Day, birthday or thank you gift.

Seasonal leaves

The red metallic bag came with a pre-printed/ embossed mistletoe design, which has been embellished with quilled mistletoe leaves and berries (see page 112), positioned directly over the existing motifs. A classic design for a Christmas gift for someone special.

Garlanded with love

This burgundy octagonal-shaped gift box has been decorated with trails of quilled ivy (see page 112) coming up from the base as though it is creeping over it, with a gold circle on the lid, again with an ivy embellishment. The tag features a scrolled heart made from ivory paper (see page 51). Use for a festive gift for a loved one or for a couple getting married at Christmas.

Alpha baby

Ready-made bright blue cardboard letters have been glued in a diagonal line to the centre of this bought baby's keepsake box. Two sets of quilled baby feet (see page 55) in a matching colour have then been added on the other diagonal as a simple yet effective decorative device.

Age spotting

This spotted gift bag has been quickly and easily enhanced by gluing open coils to some of the printed motifs. A simple circle tag has then been decorated with a quilled number 4 (see page 104). Several of these would make great party bags for a children's birthday; the number can be changed according to the birthday boy or girl's age.

Frilled to thrill

A gold bag with a printed leaf design is decorated with three frilly flowers (see page 44) made from paper graduating in colour across its width, so that the fringed tips stand out in white. This gorgeous gift packaging would be suitable for a variety of occasions, from Easter to an anniversary.

Templates

Box (page 19)

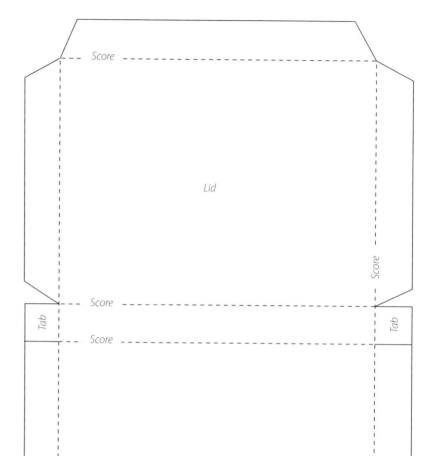

Score

Lid

Score

Score

Tab

Score

Tab

Base

Score

Tab

Score

Tab

Sweet peas (page 25)

Pea pod

Carrot cupcake (page 25) and Candle cupcake (page 105)

Cupcake

Trusty trowel and fork (page 26)

Trowel blade

Fork blade

Timeless topiary (page 28)

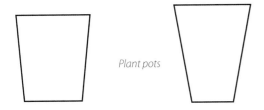

Plant pots

Handy secateurs (page 29)

Secateurs blade

Shear delight (page 29)

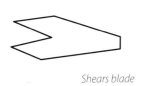

Shears blade

Insect jar (page 33)

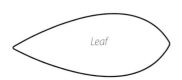

Leaf

Hovering dragonfly (page 36)

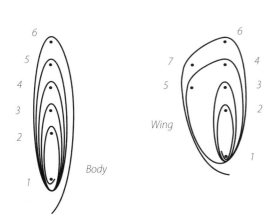

6
5
4
3
2
1

Body

7
6
5
4
3
2
1

Wing

Spotty buggy (page 56)

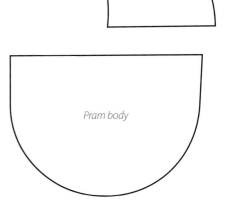

Pram hood

Pram body

Fairy queen (page 60)

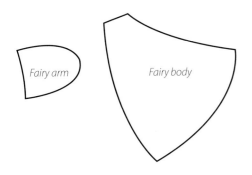

Fairy arm

Fairy body

Ornamental fan (page 69)

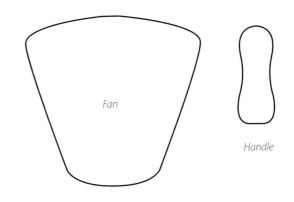

Fan

Handle

Tendril-trimmed hat (page 76)

Feathered hat (page 77)

Trendy bag (page 79)

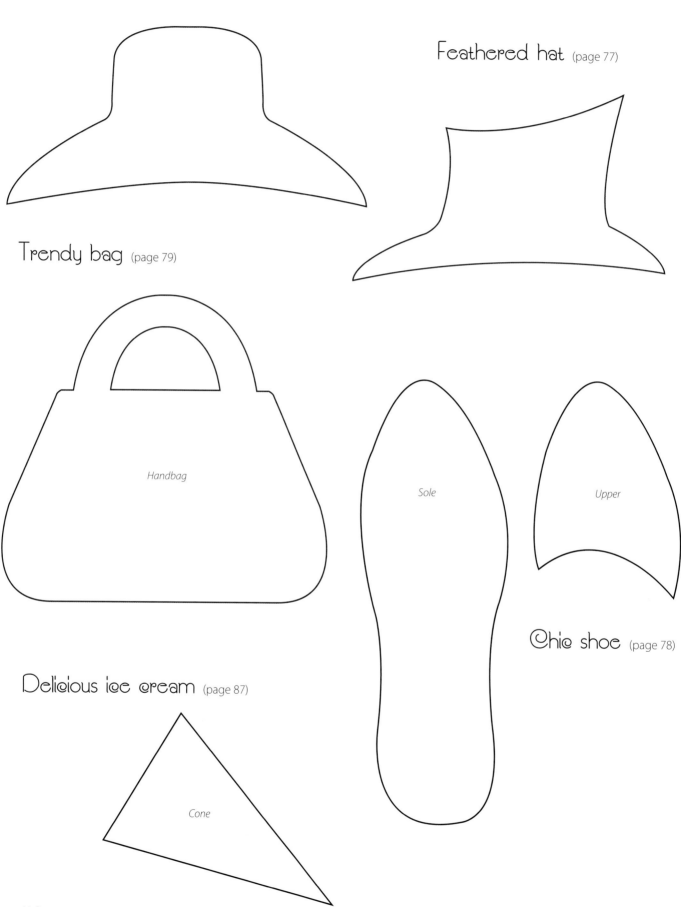

Handbag

Sole

Upper

Chic shoe (page 78)

Delicious ice cream (page 87)

Cone

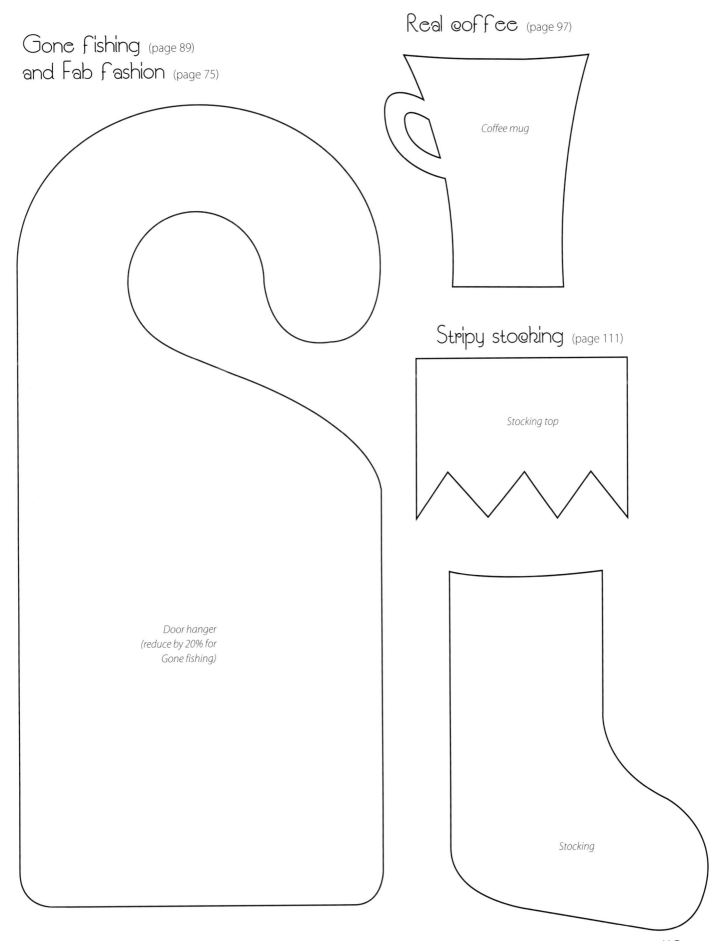

Gone fishing (page 89)
and Fab fashion (page 75)

Real coffee (page 97)

Coffee mug

Stripy stocking (page 111)

Stocking top

*Door hanger
(reduce by 20% for
Gone fishing)*

Stocking

Suppliers and materials

UK

DoCrafts (trade only)
www.docrafts.co.uk
For suppliers of quilling materials including quilling boards

Evie's Crafts Ltd
79 Dale Street
Milnrow
Rochdale
OL16 3NJ
Tel: 01706 712489
www.eviescraftsltd.co.uk
For quilling papers and supplies

Fred Aldous Ltd
37 Lever Street
Manchester
M1 1LW
Tel: 0161 236 4224
www.fredaldous.co.uk
For quilling kits and supplies

Jane Jenkins Quilling Design
33 Mill Rise
Skidby
Cottingham
HU16 5UA
Tel: 01482 843721
www.jjquilling.co.uk
For all quilling supplies

Lakeland Ltd
Alexandra Buildings
Windermere
Cumbria
LA23 1BQ
Tel: 01539 488100
www.lakeland.co.uk
For quilling boards and materials

Pebeo UK Ltd
PO Box 282
Southampton
SO45 5XD
Tel: 0808 234 2290
www.pebeo.com
For 3-D paint

USA

Crafter's Companion International
5703 Red Bug Lake Road
Winter Springs, FL 32708
Tel: 1800 399 5035
www.crafterscompanion.com
For envelope makers

Lake City Crafts
1209 Eaglecrest Street
P O Box 2009
Nixa, Missouri 65714
Tel: 417 725 8444
www.quilling.com
For fringing tools and supplies

Michaels Stores Inc
Attn: Customer Service
8000 Bent Branch Dr
Irving, TX 75063
Tel: 1 800 642 4235
www.michaels.com
General craft store chain

Quilled Creations
PO Box 492
Penfield, NY 14526
Tel: 585 388 0706
www.quilledcreations.com
For all quilling supplies

Ranger Industries Inc
15 Park Road
Tinton Falls, NJ 07724
Tel: 732 389 3535
www.rangerink.com
For Perfect Pearls™

Australia

Jonathan Mayne
P O Box 345
Mt Martha
Victoria 3934
Tel: (03) 5988 4099
www.jonathanmayne.com.au
For fringing tools and papers

Europe

Kars
P O Box 97
4050 EB Ochten
The Netherlands
Tel: 31 (0) 344 642864
www.kars.nl
For ready-fringed papers

Acknowledgments

Many thanks to Jane Trollope, Emily Rae and Eleanor Stafford at David & Charles and special thanks to Jo Richardson, Karl Adamson, Kim Sayer, Selina Jackson and my friends and family.

For further papercrafting ideas, information about the author and details of her forthcoming workshops see www.elizabethmoad.com.

Index